PURPLE PRIDE

A HIGH SCHOOL
COACH'S JOURNEY

DONALD HERMAN

Book Design by Daniel J. Adams.

Front Cover Photo by Ralph Stewart, MV Times.

Back Cover Photo by Randi Baird, Vineyard Gazette.

ISBN: 9781793925510

Printed in the United States of America.

Dedication

With love to my two families, my personal one and my extended football one. I would not have been able to accomplish all I did without your years of sacrifice and support.

FOREWORD

In the spring of 1988, I knew our school would be hiring a new physical education teacher and head football coach. During the screening process of applicants, I was asked to review all candidates' written applications. Following my examining Donald Herman's background, I decided I had to meet him.

We met for lunch and I began my initial study of the teacher who could replace me as I was about to step away temporarily for a year's leave of absence.

As our conversation unfolded, I became more and more convinced to suggest that our school administration "stop the search." Without question, he was who we wanted. And the final product of our initial lunch meeting resulted (in part) in his being hired.

Teaching and coaching mean communicating ideas. He convinced me right away that he was the ideal candidate.

We spoke of goals and he felt it best when his players write down their individual and team goals. Doing this, he then said they would share them with others.

Listening to his teaching and coaching background I discovered that he knew that getting good at anything required unrelenting work habits and a total focus. I learned that any success he had would be shared team-wide and that he was a coach who had never strained for the spotlight. Although his teams received much well-deserved recognition, he acknowledged that newspaper headlines yellow fast. The final product was the athlete's well-being. In looking back over his long-lasting teaching career, it was clear that Donald Herman was a coach full of compassion and wisdom.

One of the factors that I have used consistently in judging a coach was whether or not I'd want my high school sons to play for him. I'd want to know if my sons would be treated fairly and would eventually walk away from their playing careers claiming that playing for him was rewarding and loaded with positive life-long memories.

Yes, he more than met all those expectations over our three decades together. As a long-time varsity basketball coach here on the Martha's Vineyard, I saw him up close and realized that we shared the same philosophies and approaches while coaching our athletes. As his coaching stories are shared in this upcoming collection of his career, the readers will quickly learn how this man earned the island-wide respect we all show for his efforts.

Thanks, Donald, for sharing these wonderful stories and may they serve as lessons for future coaches of any sports at any level.

I'm always been proud to call Coach Herman a longtime friend and fellow teacher/coach. May we share many more productive lunches together.

Jay Schofield
Varsity Basketball Coach
Martha's Vineyard Regional High School

CHAPTER 1

"Your destiny is the story of your life, and you get to tell the story your way. Of course, life is full of many variables beyond our control, but at the end of the day, you determine the actions that influence your path." - Scott Allan

At the time I did not know it, but in my second year of college, my career path became evident when a high school classmate, David Roberts, asked me to help him coach a youth football team.

Born in Savannah, Georgia, I grew up the youngest of three children to Samuel and Archee Herman. My childhood home was within 100 yards of Hull Park, where I was first introduced to organized sports and which doubled as my babysitter. Often I was called home from the park for dinner, as day turned into night. It did not matter what sport was in season; growing up, I tried them all. Baseball was a favorite but I developed a real love of football, which in the south is the king of sports. A common expression where I come from is, "There are two sports seasons in the south--football and spring football." I fondly remember taking batting practice during my high school baseball seasons while wearing my football practice pants. We had three weeks of spring football practice at the start of baseball season each year. I took batting practice, shagged some ground balls as I played second base, and then went to two hours or so of football practice.

My father, also born in Savannah, graduated from Duke University with a degree in business. During World War II, he served in the Army as a captain in the European theater. My father was never sick when I was young. In fact, whenever he had a headache, he merely rubbed Ben-Gay on his forehead instead of taking any over-the-counter medicine. Maybe that is why I always told my players, when they were feeling pain to rub some dirt on it, one of my father's favorite remedies if any of us ever suffered a minor injury. However, when he was a child, he contracted rheumatic fever, which would impact his health later in life.

During my junior year of college, my father had the first of his four open heart surgeries to replace his leaky mitral valve, a byproduct of his rheumatic fever earlier in life. The first two replacement valves were pigskin valves. The running joke about why those pigskin valves failed was because my father was Jewish so his body rejected them. The surgeon used a metallic valve in the third surgery. The fourth surgery was done to repair some stitching from the previous operation. Four times he survived having his sternum sawed through, ribs spread open, and placed on the heart-lung machine. All of these surgeries took place within a ten year span. Although he survived each surgery physically, the vascular strain of being on and off the heart-lung machine did irreparable damage to my father mentally. He never returned to the man he was before that first operation.

My father was an avid sports fan. As a senior in high school, he was the Savannah tennis champion with bulging scrapbooks of news articles about him, his teammates, and the tennis superstars of the day but I never saw him play. However, my sister, who played tennis, remembers hitting with him one night on a local court. Daddy particularly loved football and baseball. We spent many hours talking about and watching sports on television together. There is a scene from the movie, *Field of Dreams*, that reminds me of my father. Ray Kinsella, played by Kevin Costner, asked his father if he wanted to "have a catch." That scene never fails to bring tears to my eyes. My father and I spent endless hours playing catch in our front yard when I was a child. He never missed any of my games in any sport and was usually one of the parents who drove other teammates to games. Samuel Herman passed away on February 3, 1993, at the age of seventy-five. February 3rd is also my brother's birthday. Sadly, he never saw me coach a game at Martha's Vineyard Regional High School, which I know would have made him happy.

My mother, Archee, was born in Hershey, Pennsylvania two weeks after her father passed away. She was brought back to Savannah with her mother when she was old enough to travel and stayed for the remainder of her life. Archee was named with a spelling twist for her father, Archie, who tragically, she never knew. She was a stay-at-home mom for most of my childhood and was always involved in charitable, community organizations. When we got older, she went to work as a buyer and sales manager for children and teen clothing stores. Mama was always there for her three children and husband. On game days she prepared home cooked, pregame meals which typically consisted of a tossed salad, T-bone steak, baked potato, and sweet iced tea. Sometimes she cooked these meals during her lunch break from work. If any of us children ever had a friend who needed a meal, Mama always made sure they were well-fed. She looked out for all of our friends as if they were family. If any of her children or our friends needed parental advice, she made herself available. My mother rarely missed any of my games and was the one who could be heard yelling encouragement or advice from the bleachers. She was knowledgeable about sports and would have made a good coach. Archee Herman passed away on November 2, 1998 at the age of seventy-one. Mama saw me coach three games at Martha's Vineyard, two of which we won.

My brother Bobby, eight years my elder, had always helped me in sports and also played baseball and football. Midway through his sophomore year of high school, he transferred from a public school to Benedictine Military School, a private, military, all male Catholic high school. Because of this transfer, Bobby was ineligible to play football his junior year.

Bobby coached me in youth football that one year, while I was playing on the Panthers. I played for the Panthers for five years, and we never won a game. We never even came close to winning. The coaches considered me the best running back on the team, which wasn't saying much because we rarely scored any points. My strengths were on the defensive side of the ball.

I remember one game in particular when I was in the sixth grade. We were losing 35-0 with two minutes left. I had been taken out of the game to let others play. The cheerleaders started one of their cheers, "That's alright, that's okay, we're gonna beat them anyway." Are you kidding me? What game were they watching?

My sister, Barbara, five years older, was also there supporting me.

Barbara, who was always interested in how her little brother was doing, was also an athlete. She was a talented ballet dancer. She may have been able to make a career out of dancing but chose another direction. Barbara wasn't home often when I was in high school or college. She moved to Chicago, married, and then moved to suburban Philadelphia. While raising her children, she gave up her toe shoes for a tennis racquet and aerobics. You could say, we all had the athletic gene and love of sports passed down to us from our parents.

After leaving the Panthers, an experience I would not trade for the world, I played my junior high years on an all-star team. Brothers Chuck and Don Stewart coached the team. My coaches gave me my lifelong nickname, "Stump," due to the fact I was built like a tree stump. I enjoyed success those two years as we won most of our games, a new experience for me, at least in football.

Like my brother, I attended Benedictine Military School. We were referred to as BC because our nickname was the cadets. A long-standing memory was my first football meeting in the high school freshman locker room. As I walked in, I noticed that I was one of 100 or more other freshmen trying out for the team. We had just 126 boys in the entire freshman class. Our coaches made cuts from the 100 players trying out, down to just thirty-five. I was fortunate not only to make the team but was named a defensive starter at nose guard. Tall genes do not run in my family. I am not a big person. At that time in my life, I was about 5' tall and maybe weighed 140 pounds, but I was quick and aggressive. Our freshman team enjoyed the school's first undefeated season and won the city championship.

While in high school at BC, I played football for Jim Walsh. Coach Walsh had a tremendous impact on my coaching style and philosophy. In fact, he was the one who suggested I go into teaching and coaching. He took over a fledgling football program at BC in 1970. His first team went 8-2. The worst record I experienced while playing for Coach Walsh was in my junior year, going 7-3. Jim Walsh was the head coach at BC for twenty-five years but continued working there for nearly fifteen more years before retiring. He is still one of the winningest football coaches from Savannah. The Greater Savannah Athletic Hall of Fame inducted Coach Jim Walsh in 1997.

I played with several Division I college football players, a couple of whom went on to play in the NFL and USFL. Some of my teammates played at the University of Alabama, the University of Georgia, Georgia Tech, and the University of South Carolina. Four of my teammates played on National Championship teams while at Alabama and Georgia. I competed against athletes who played at the Division I level at UCLA and Arizona. They, too, played pro football for the Houston Oilers, Miami Dolphins, and the Philadelphia Eagles. I mention this to point out that I saw some talented players during my high school years and later. When asked if I thought any of my Vineyard players could play at the Division I level and beyond, I always thought about those athletes.

There are some great men I played for and learned from in my childhood years. Billy Green, a sergeant on the Savannah police force, was my little league baseball coach for four years. When I was twelve, my team won the city championship. Tom Moore and Luke Sims coached me while playing for the Panthers. I've already mentioned the impact the Stewart brothers and Jim Walsh had on me. John Stephens was my defensive coordinator at BC for three years. John was the first coach to introduce me to the importance of weight training.

Along with parents who took great pride in my accomplishments, I was fortunate to be coached by great men who valued winning but also emphasized the teaching of fundamentals, sportsmanship, and hard work. They also stressed having fun while accomplishing all of the above. My coaches worked us hard in practice and during games, but their personalities were such that you enjoyed being around them and playing for them. I wanted my athletes to feel the same way about playing for me.

My experience in youth sports and involvement with great coaches and role models are among the many things that went into making the final version of the football coach and man I later became. They believed, as I do, in old-fashioned, hard-nosed football and ethics. Whenever I was confronted with tough decisions, I always reverted to the lessons learned from my parents, my coaches, and my broad spectrum of athletic experiences.

Immediately after college graduation, I was hired to teach and coach football at Jenkins High School in Savannah. Don Stewart, one of my junior high coaches, had become the principal at Jenkins. I worked at

Jenkins for four years. However, after my third year, Bob Herndon, the head coach, left Savannah for a head coaching position near Atlanta. I applied for the head job but did not get hired. Rick Tomberlin was hired as the new head coach at Jenkins. He was a year older than I and had one year of being a high school head football coach at a small school in Georgia. Remaining in my position as defensive coordinator under Rick, we went 8-3, losing in the first round of the playoffs.

That spring I was fired by Rick as his defensive coordinator. His reason for firing me was that our coaching philosophies were *different*. I thought about staying on at Jenkins as just a teacher but that was the same time the head football job at Johnson High School in Savannah became available. Alexander Graham Bells' saying, "When one door closes another one opens," applies here. I was hired at Johnson and had three enjoyable years there. We played Jenkins each year, soundly beating them in the last two of those three years.

In 1988, three years after being the head football coach at Johnson High School in Savannah, Martha's Vineyard gave me the opportunity to become their head football coach and physical education teacher. For the next twenty-eight years, I taught and coached football and other sports on the Vineyard before retiring in June of 2016. My career spanned thirty-five years.

I coached outstanding young men and had talented assistant coaches at Martha's Vineyard Regional High School. Both groups made me a better coach. Several of those football players went on to have successful college careers, both academically and athletically, in various divisions. Among the most notable are Todd Araujo, Class of 1990. After graduation, Todd played at The College of Holy Cross in Worcester, Massachusetts. Todd would go on to become a General Law Practitioner in Juneau, Alaska. Jason Dyer, Class of 1993, was a three-year starter at quarterback. In his junior and senior years, he helped lead those teams to a 21-2 record, back-to-back Mayflower League and Super Bowl Championships. Jason would go on to play quarterback at Fitchburg State University and set numerous school passing records. Hans Buder, Class of 2004, also played quarterback for me and was his class' Valedictorian. In addition to being a solid athlete, he was also quite compassionate. When Hans was a freshman at Duke University, he traveled to New Orleans to offer help and aid after

Hurricane Katrina. Another outstanding scholar/athlete was Michael McCarthy, class of 2009, who started at quarterback his four years at Bridgewater State College. After graduation he played a year of professional football in Europe for the Geneva Seahawks and for a year of Arena Football. Finally, Randall Jette, class of 2011, was our high school's first FBS (Football Bowl Subdivision) full-scholarship recipient. He started all four years at cornerback for UMASS Amherst, after being red-shirted in his first year. Randall became an undrafted, free agent, defensive back for the Green Bay Packers in 2016 but was later released.

In April of 2015, I was inducted into the Massachusetts High School Football Coaches Hall of Fame. I was grateful for this honor. This recognition would have never happened without the help and support of so many people. Unfortunately, my parents were not alive to see their son accomplish this achievement.

If not for the support and encouragement from my parents, siblings, and my wife Pam, my career would not have been nearly as successful.

As a consequence of my career choices, my immediate family sacrificed so much while I was coaching. Pam raised our three children, Eric, Adam, and Gail, especially focusing on their needs during their younger years while I was unable to be there. Due to my all-consuming football schedule, I missed being able to watch my children participate in some of their activities.

The experiences in this book are just a few small selections from my twenty-eight years of coaching football at Martha's Vineyard.

CHAPTER 2

"Good things come to those who wait... greater things come to those who get off their ass and do anything to make it happen." - Unknown

Everyone's lives are full of important decisions that can determine a future path. There are two specific choices I made that set my life on this path.

Growing up, my family always ate dinner together. This tradition continued on Sunday nights, even after I was no longer living in my parents' house. My brother and sister-in-law, who lived in Savannah, would attend these weekly meals.

In the fall of 1982, I was in my second year of teaching and coaching football at Jenkins High School and in my first of three years as the defensive coordinator.

It was a typical Sunday night dinner at my parents' house. At some time during the meal, my sister-in-law, Linda, said, "Donald, there is a cute young teacher at my school. Would you be interested in going on a blind date with her?"

After thinking about it for a brief moment, I told her, "I've never been on a blind date, but if you think she is cute, then I'm game." That was the end of the conversation.

At our next Sunday dinner, I asked Linda what happened with her teacher-friend. Linda said that she asked and Pam had said she wasn't interested at that time. I didn't think any more about it.

At the following Sunday dinner, Linda once again brought up the blind date. She said, "Pam has reconsidered and is now interested in going out with you." Linda gave me Pam's telephone number and the following Tuesday night, I called her. Noticing her northern accent on the other end, I asked where she was from and she said Martha's Vineyard. I asked, "Where is that? I've never heard of Martha's Vineyard."

Following our pleasant conversation, I asked her out for a rather unconventional first date. She said yes. Jenkins would play a rare Saturday afternoon game with a 5:00 p.m. kickoff. I made arrangements for Bobby and Linda to drive her to the game. Before our kickoff, I saw the three of them walk into the stadium and went over to introduce myself. I remember thinking to myself, "Linda was right, Pam is cute." They sat together during the game, which our team won 35-0. Afterward, we all went to a party at the house I had been renting with two other male friends.

After our first date, I asked Pam to go on a more traditional date; dinner and a movie. I took her to one of my favorite restaurants but we never made it to the movie. We stayed at the restaurant talking. Pam often reminds me that I did most of the talking. It was then I learned that Pam didn't like football.

I fell for her hook, line, and sinker. It was easy being with Pam. She was down to earth, smart, and had a great sense of humor. I also found out why Pam at first said "no" to the blind date. She was shown a picture of me, which I admit was not flattering. Though I never considered myself handsome, the ugly, unstylish glasses I was wearing in the photo did nothing to enhance my appearance. Fortunately, Pam had heard some nice things about me. She was told I was a kind and considerate person. Those comments are what changed her mind.

Pam and I dated for three months before I asked her to marry me. Again, she said yes. Our first date, the blind one, was on October 16, 1982. We were engaged on January 16, 1983. We were both twenty-five when we were married on Martha's Vineyard on June 23, 1984.

Pam and I would continue to live and work in Savannah. She continued teaching at Mercer Middle School and I eventually became head football coach at Johnson High School. We bought a house and planned on settling down in Savannah.

On January 23, 1987, our lives changed forever when our son, Eric, was born. That previous fall, our team had just completed a very successful football season going 7-3. Those seven wins were a school record for most wins in a season and I was named the Savannah Football Coach of the Year.

Pam and I both thought that if we were ever going to leave Savannah, now was the time. I started applying for other teaching and coaching jobs. I had several interviews in Massachusetts, Georgia, Virginia, and North Carolina, but nothing ever came of them, though a few schools made offers. There were no teaching jobs to go along with the coaching, so we stayed another year in Savannah.

That spring, Pam received word from her cousin on Martha's Vineyard that a high school PE teaching position and the head football position were going to be advertised. Pam did some early checking and discovered the teaching piece was a one-year-only position. Still, I decided to put in my application and was one of three finalists interviewed for the teaching/coaching position. I came to Martha's Vineyard in May of 1988 to tour the school and have my interview. I met with several students and finished the day with a really positive feeling about the job on Martha's Vineyard.

Roughly a week after my interview, I received a phone call from Roger Lemenager, the head of the interview committee, informing me that I was being offered the positions, which I accepted. Naturally, I was very excited, but Pam was even more so. She was going home.

Early that June I flew back to the Vineyard to meet my players and to start putting together a coaching staff. I also wanted to meet Jay Schofield. Jay was the PE teacher who was taking a one-year leave of absence. I needed to know what his thoughts were about returning to the Vineyard the following year. The two of us met for lunch at the Artcliff Diner, a local restaurant in Vineyard Haven, one of the six towns on MV. We hit it off right away. Jay had been a successful boys' varsity basketball and girls' varsity soccer coach and seemed to be rather unique. He and his wife, Pat, another PE teacher at the West Tisbury School, were taking a year off to try a new career.

The decision to move to Martha's Vineyard was not made easily. In Savannah, we owned a house, both had teaching jobs, Eric was eighteen months old, and we were expecting our second child the following February. We had to sell our house and find an affordable place to rent on the Vineyard. Pam decided to stay home, care for our children, and take in one or two other children to make ends meet. This was to be a serious life-changing move. If we made the move to Martha's Vineyard and the Schofields decided to return, I would be out of a job. We both decided it was a risk worth taking.

We moved to Martha's Vineyard at the beginning of August 1988. Pam's father, Stan Mercer, flew to Savannah to drive one of our two cars back. Being pregnant, Pam and Eric flew to Martha's Vineyard. In my car, I had our two pets. We had a cat, Shnookums, and a small dog, Apollo.

Pam, Eric, and I moved three times in the first two months. We rented a house together with Pam's brother and his young family for the first three weeks. We lived with my in-laws for one week. Then we rented a house owned by one of my assistants for the month of September. The house we were to rent year-round would not be available until October. It was a hectic two months for us. I was starting a new teaching job and coaching football. Pam was taking care of Eric, caring for two other children, and she was pregnant. The majority of our belongings were locked up in a storage unit on the Vineyard. Eventually, we were able to get settled for the year.

On February 13th, 1989, our second child, Adam, was born.

The Schofields returned the next year. I took another one-year-only teaching job at the high school, teaching two geography classes and three PE classes. At the end of that year teaching geography, I apologized to my students as I felt I didn't do a great job. I coached football and baseball, the other sport I love.

Just before the third year, the geography teacher returned. Once again I was hired for a one-year-only teaching position. I started the year teaching PE, basic math, and coaching football and baseball. However, after the first three weeks of that third year, our athletic director, Mark McCarthy, decided to take a job in Connecticut. I became the school's athletic director, continued teaching three PE classes, and coached football, but I had to give up coaching a spring sport.

After four years in those positions, I was given a choice. The school's enrollment was increasing, and the high school was making a move to a full-time athletic director. I was asked if I wanted to be a full-time AD or a full-time PE teacher and I said, "Thank you very much. I'll take the full-time PE teaching position."

What began as a one-and-done year turned into a wonderful, twenty-eight-year teaching and coaching career on Martha's Vineyard.

I was the third coach in the history of Martha's Vineyard Regional High School to be inducted into the state's Hall of Fame, following Robert Nute, the girls' basketball coach, and Jay Schofield. They were both inducted into their respective Massachusetts Basketball Halls of Fame.

With one season left before retiring in June of 2016, after being a head football coach for thirty-one years, my teams would finish with 232 wins and 109 losses, and play in eight Super Bowls, winning five. This record includes my three years as the head coach at Johnson High School in Savannah.

There is no way my incredible life and career would have been possible had I not gone on that blind date in 1982. Pam and I had three beautiful children. Our daughter, Gail, was born March 14th, 1992. Martha's Vineyard proved to be a great place to raise a family and a beautiful place to work and live.

My message to young people is, "Never be afraid to take a chance on yourself. If you don't believe in yourself, who will."

CHAPTER 3

"Motivation is simple. You eliminate those that aren't." - Lou Holtz

As the newly hired head coach I wanted to meet my players before school let out for the summer. We met in a classroom at the end of a school day. I remember there were roughly thirty-five boys, students from 9th through 11th grades, in attendance.

I gave a brief introduction of myself and handed out a 3x5 index card to each person. On one side of the card, I asked each player to write his top three individual and team goals for the upcoming season. Almost every player's number one team goal was to beat Nantucket. On the opposite side of the card I asked each player to value from 1 to 10 the priorities I had listed on the blackboard, such as family, school, friends, football and religion. I hoped that "football" would be somewhere in the top four of each player's priorities, assuming that the higher football ranked, the easier my job would be that first year. I let the students know that writing their name on the card was optional. I was happy to see that the majority of players ranked football in the top four of their priorities.

Once the activity cards were collected for my later viewing, I reviewed my team rules and expectations. One of the rules I discussed that day was my position on hair, both on their heads and faces. One of my steadfast rules was that no hair was to extend below the helmet nor was facial hair, other than a mustache, allowed. I'm old-school and like the old-school look. More importantly, this rule was instated so that a player would have to sacrifice something he wanted. I reasoned that if a player cut his hair, when he wanted it long, that he was all-in for the program. That was an easy rule to enforce because the long hair fad of the 70's had gone out of fashion, with one exception. It was apparent that Matt Borkow was a lineman. He was roughly six-feet tall and weighed around 250 pounds. A well-built young man and a smart student, Matt had varsity playing experience and was liked by all. Matt, whose long, flowing locks went well below his shoulders, approached me as I was leaving the classroom and asked if we could talk. Being of Jewish lineage (a heritage we shared), he was given the nickname, "Flying Jew," by his peers. Matt started the conversation by congratulating me on my new position. He said that my rules were good ones, but continued, "I don't see how the length of my hair has any impact on my ability to play football."

I replied, "This is an important rule of mine. If a player is willing to sacrifice something he likes, just to play football, then he is more willing to do what is needed for the team to be successful." I also informed him, "Your hair will impact your playing because if you don't conform, you don't play." I then told him, "This is a great opportunity for you to stand out and become a true team leader. If you cut your hair, other players will see this sacrifice, and you will gain instant respect from everyone." With that, I shook Matt's hand and left for my in-law's house.

Within two hours of leaving the school, there was a phone call for me. It was Matt. How he got my in-laws' phone number, I'm not entirely sure. Remember, I did tell you earlier that Matt was smart. Matt proceeded to tell me, "I thought about your hair rule and talked things over with my Mom and decided that I want to play football. I will cut my hair to your specifications." I thanked Matt for the phone call and congratulated him on taking the first step toward becoming a leader.

My first football team on the Vineyard, the 1988 team, would finish the season at 5-5, improving on the previous year's record. No, we did not beat Nantucket that year, losing 14-0 for my first of many games against our "sister" island. However, because of players like Matt, we had established the foundation of a respected and successful program.

CHAPTER 4

"Sports do not build character. They reveal it." - John Wooden

During my first spring on Martha's Vineyard, I was the boys' track coach. Joe Schroder was the girls' coach. I had never played or coached track, so Joe and I split the coaching duties. I coached the throwers while Joe coached the runners.

Based on my years as a football coach, I have a strong belief in conditioning. That was one area I felt comfortable with while coaching track that year.

The boys' and girls' track teams often ran meets together. However, for one meet, at Harwich High School in Harwich, Massachusetts, only the boys were running. The last two events of the day were the relays. We ran the 4x4 relay first and then the 4x1 relay. The 4x4 has four runners completing one full lap around the track, one runner at a time. The 4x1 has four runners each completing a quarter lap around the track. Each runner must complete a successful baton exchange to a teammate before running. We were poised to win the meet that day, but needed to win both relays. I felt that our 4x1 would win. The question was, how would our 4x4 do?

Heading into the third leg of the 4x4, Harwich had a commanding lead. With their quarter lap lead, the outcome for us looked bleak. At that point, junior, Ricky Duarte received the baton. Ricky was tall and thin and built to run. He took off sprinting the entire lap. At the halfway point, he began to close the gap. As Ricky headed toward the final exchange, the Vineyard held a slight lead. Ricky not only caught Harwich but passed them. Due to his efforts, we won the 4x4 and 4x1 and went on to win the meet.

I gained a great deal of respect for the young man that day. Ricky did not play football during my first year of coaching at MV. He did, however, play his senior year. Ricky was a huge reason we enjoyed the success we did in 1989, going 9-1 and setting a record for most wins in a single season, up to that point.

Two other memorable Ricky Duarte stories took place in 1989. The first was when our team was working on a two minute, offensive drill. Ricky fumbled the ball, but instead of jumping on the ball, he just stood there looking at the ball on the ground. I almost lost it on Ricky. When I saw another offensive player recover the ball, with Ricky still standing there, I yelled to the player, "Give me the ball." I got Ricky's attention by first throwing the ball roughly ten yards away and yelling at Ricky, "Get on the ball." As Ricky recovered that ball, I had him quickly throw me the ball. I threw the ball roughly ten yards in another direction. Again, I yelled at Ricky, "Get on the ball." I repeated this fumble recovery drill for all to see. This made a lasting impression on Ricky and the rest of the team. Never again in that year, would the ball stay on the ground without a Vineyard player fighting to recover it. I have repeated this drill from time to time during my career, and each time the unfortunate player and team learned a valuable lesson.

The second Ricky story happened during a Friday pregame practice. That year we ran the double slot, option style offense. The double slot offense consists of one split end receiver and one running back aligned just off the offensive tackle, on both sides of the ball. Senior Todd Araujo at QB led us. Todd is one of the best athletes I have ever coached. We also had the perfect, high school, option fullback: senior, Louis Paciello. Both Todd and Louis were recognized as the unofficial team and school leaders. In those days I did not have season captains. Instead, I looked for all my seniors to be leaders, rotating seniors as weekly captains.

We were doing a passing drill that had our receivers running their pass routes on air. That means there is no defense. As the receivers were running their routes, I called out one of their names. That receiver knew the pass was coming to him. The QB was to throw the ball to the receiver whose name I called.

The drill was going well. We had been running this drill for about five minutes and had a very high completion percentage. The QB was able to locate the designated receiver and deliver the ball to him. Then it was Ricky's turn. Ricky was one of our slot receiver/ running backs. As Ricky ran his route, I called out his name. Instead of Ricky turning to locate the ball, as he did earlier in the drill, he stopped, looked my way, and yelled out, "What?" As he yelled, Todd had thrown the ball. The ball hit Ricky squarely in the back of the helmet. In amazement we all looked at Ricky. In disbelief, I asked him, "Why do you think I've been calling out receiver's names for the past five minutes?"

Ricky just looked at me, dropped his head and said, "I know coach. I'm an idiot." The entire team and coaching staff just burst out laughing.

There is a saying, "Never assume, for when you do assume, you often make an ass-out-of-you-and-me." Even though we had been performing that drill for five minutes, I assumed that when I called out Ricky's name, he would know what was happening. I assumed wrong. I'm just glad we ran that drill while wearing helmets.

CHAPTER 5

"Life is truly known only to those who suffer, lose, endure adversity and stumble from defeat to defeat." - Anais Nin

My good friend and co-worker, Jay Schofield, often said, "Healthy choices and sober fun." The PE staff would often use this saying as our students left our class. We wanted each student to make smart, healthy decisions while still having sober fun in their daily lives.

The 1991 football team, following a 4-6 record the previous year, was in its second week of summer practice. We had several key starters returning and appeared ready to compete for the Mayflower League Championship and first ever Super Bowl berth.

That year the Massachusetts Interscholastic Athletic Association, MIAA, established a new football playoff system for the Super Bowl. The new system was arranged so that each league champion would qualify for the postseason and compete against another league champion in their Divisional Super Bowl game. Eastern Massachusetts consisted of six divisions and each division had four leagues. Our league, the Mayflower League, was matched up with one of the Boston City School leagues for our Super Bowl.

One of our returning players was junior, OG/LB, Sam Hayes. Sam was a short, fast, physical, emotional player; my kind of high school football player. During this time, Sam had an older girlfriend who was scheduled to leave for college on the evening of one of our double session practice days. Sam asked me, the morning before his girlfriend was to leave for college, if he could have permission to be fifteen minutes late to the evening practice. He wanted to go to the boat to bid her farewell. Keep in mind that Martha's Vineyard is an island and the boat ride to Woods Hole in Falmouth is forty-five minutes each way. I told Sam, "No. I expect you to be on time to practice, along with the rest of your teammates." I suggested that he spend time that day with her, take her out for breakfast or lunch after the morning session, help her pack, and just spend quality time together. I restated that I did expect him to be at practice and on time that evening. Sam told me that he would do the things I suggested and that he would be at practice on time that night. The discussion was over.

Our next practice started at 5:30 p.m., and Sam was nowhere to be found. After some quick and easy checking, I discovered that Sam, did indeed, take the boat ride with his girlfriend. Sam missed the entire practice. You can only imagine how angry and disappointed I was with Sam and his choice. After that evening's practice, I called the seniors together. I told them what had happened and let them know we had a decision to make. Would we keep Sam on the team or kick him off for lying to me and forsaking his squad for his individual needs? The seniors voted. Some seniors wanted Sam off the team, but the majority of them felt he should continue playing. Regardless, I needed to make an example out of him. When Sam showed up for practice the next morning, I asked him what had happened. He told me, "Coach, I planned on just going to the boat to see my girlfriend leave and then come to practice. But, due to traffic, I got to the boat late. I said screw it and went over on the boat with her."

I made Sam meet with the seniors before the morning practice began. The night before, I had taken some time deciding Sam's high school football fate. That summer the game field had not been mowed. Why I don't know, but the field looked more like a hay field than a football field. Finally, I arrived at a decision that involved giving Sam a choice: Option #1: Quit the team. Option #2: Mow the field, with a push mower. If he chose Option #2, Sam had a two-day window to finish, because the start of school was approaching. He would not have time during the school day to get the needed work finished. He chose to mow the field. A custodian provided the mower and gas. It took Sam nearly twelve hours to complete the job, but he did finish. He learned a valuable lesson that week and in his own words, "You see it wasn't about me, never was, nor is football. It was about letting down my teammates, putting myself first, and the real underlying message I carry with me to this day... Never look a man in the eye, give him your word and then break it. It's not about you."

Fast forward that season to the Island Cup game, which is played the Saturday before Thanksgiving. Martha's Vineyard would host Nantucket. The winner would be Mayflower League Champion and receive an automatic berth to the Super Bowl.

Both teams entered the game with 9-1 records, as we had each lost our first game of the season. The weekend before the Nantucket game, Sam told me, "Coach, I had a premonition. When I look up into the bleachers before the game, my girlfriend is going to be in the stands cheering the Vineyard and me on to victory." Low and behold and unbeknownst to Sam, his father, Roy Hayes, bought an airline ticket for his girlfriend to fly to the Vineyard from her college in Florida. She arrived the night before the game and surprised Sam.

The 1991 team finished the season 11-1. We beat Nantucket, the defending league champs, and went on to win our first Super Bowl. Sam Hayes was a significant contributor to that team's success.

I still see Sam and he never fails to mention that substantial lesson and the wrong choice he made his junior year. When you play a team sport, everything you do must be what is best for the team, not what is best for the individual.

The lesson Sam learned will be with him the rest of his life.

CHAPTER 6

"Either love your players or get out of coaching." - Bobby Dodd

In 1978 Vineyard head football coach, John Bacheller, and Nantucket's head coach, Vito Capizzo, came up with an idea. They agreed to purchase a large trophy that the winning team would keep at their school for the year. Each game's final score would be engraved on the trophy's plaque. This marked the beginning of the Island Cup, adding to the intensity of the rivalry. There has been much discussion about who paid for the trophy. However, John has the cancelled check providing the proof that he did.

Nantucket held a lopsided advantage in wins. The Vineyard had just two wins claiming the coveted Island Cup, 1985 and 1989.

We beat Nantucket in 1989 at home, and two years later we, once again, played Nantucket at home. Our 1991 team had accomplished many things. Since losing our first game 0-6, we ran off nine straight convincing wins. This senior class would be my first four year class, and they held a special place in my heart.

The Island Cup game was a tremendous rivalry, one that both island communities supported, along with fans from across the United States. It was not uncommon for people from all over the country to attend this one game, even if they were not loyal to either island.

Before our last practice that Friday afternoon in November, I wanted to do something for my players, especially the seniors. I expected to win the game the next day, but if this would be our last practice together, I wanted the team to know how much they meant to me. At the end of practice, after bringing the team together and giving them my last talk of the day, I asked the seniors to line up on the goal line nearest our scoreboard. To the rest of the team I said, "Take a good look at those seniors. Tomorrow's game is to be played for them." I instructed each player and coach to line up at the goal line and shake each of the seniors' hands, thank them, and wish them good luck in their last Island Cup game. I went first, coaching staff behind me, followed by the remaining players. Many of my comments were personal as were the comments of the players to each other.

Quite early, as we made our way through the senior line, it became apparent what an emotional ceremony this was going to be, hugging each player and thanking them for their years of sacrifice and dedication to Vineyard football. When the tears began to well up in me, I saw the tears in the seniors' eyes as well. That team had about forty-players on the roster, which included grades 9-12. The entire senior appreciation took about fifteen minutes. After the last player went through the line and the team began to gather at midfield, the seniors huddled together and gave themselves one big hug.

Granted, this could have been all that I needed to do, but as usual, I took things a little farther than necessary. Earlier that week, I had decided to write a letter about my thoughts and feelings on the upcoming game and the players on the team. I would pick a senior to read this letter to the team. After all the players had gathered back at the fifty yard line, I handed the letter to senior Jake Borkow. I chose Jake because he suffered a broken ankle earlier in the season and wouldn't be able to play in his last Island Cup game. Plus, Jake was well-spoken and would be able to communicate my words and emotions to the rest of the team.

The coaches and I left the field as the players went into the trailer located behind the home bleachers, where we met before each game and at half-time. I do not recall exactly what was in the letter I wrote that day, but I do know that I thanked the players and wished them well, not just in football, but in life. I wanted them to realize just how much fun they would have Saturday, playing not only for themselves, but for their families, their school and their community, but most importantly, playing for each other. I urged them to have NO REGRETS.

Growing up on the Vineyard in such a small community, most of the football players had attended school together since kindergarten. Most had grown up together their entire lives. Several were related to someone else on the team. They lived next door to each other, played together on youth sports teams, and played together on playgrounds. Even their parents had gone to school together. It indeed was a family and community affair.

I don't know if the senior appreciation worked or the letter that I wrote made any profound impressions, but the Vineyard beat Nantucket that Saturday, 14-6. There were over 5,000 people in attendance, the most significant crowd to ever attend a football game on Martha's Vineyard.

This win marked some firsts: the first ten win season in the school's football history, the first outright Mayflower League championship, and the first trip to the Super Bowl. Two weeks later, the Vineyard won its first Super Bowl, defeating Jeremiah Burke High School from Boston.

A new tradition was born. From then on, on the last day of the regular season, at the end of practice, the football team's seniors would align themselves on the goal line nearest the scoreboard. All of the coaches, followed by the rest of the team members, would shake hands with the seniors, thank them for their hard work and dedication, and wish them good luck in Saturday's game. Afterward, a senior would be randomly selected to read my letter to the team.

I did not realize what this letter meant to my players until August of my last season. I was attending a twenty-first birthday party for a family friend, a former player of mine. The birthday boy, Michael Montanile, was the player I had selected to read the letter. Michael told me that he had recently come across it and that he reread the letter and had gotten emotional all over again. It was then I decided to make my last letter, the 2015 version, a parting gift for all of the seniors on that team.

Who says football coaches and players can't be emotional? I think it is essential, especially for young men, to feel comfortable showing and expressing their feelings and love for fellow male friends. Our program used the word "love" often. In fact, the emotions and connections to each of these players are still active today.

CHAPTER 7

"One thing about championship teams is that they're resilient. No matter what is thrown at them, no matter how deep the hole, they find a way to bounce back and overcome adversity." - Nick Saban

It was the 1992 version of the Island Cup game with Martha's Vineyard playing on Nantucket. My teams had beaten Nantucket twice in four years. Both teams were entering the 1992 game with equal records of 9-1. Just as in 1991, we had each lost the first game of the season, both non-league games.

It had been twenty years since Martha's Vineyard had won on Nantucket. That year, 1972, the MV team was led by Ron Brown, a standout athlete who eventually played at Brown University, had several NFL try-outs, and was a longstanding assistant coach at the University of Nebraska.

The 1992 Island Cup game had the same implications as the 1991 game. The winner would be the Mayflower League Champion and earn an automatic berth in the divisional Super Bowl game held the first Saturday in December. For the Vineyard, it was also an opportunity to end the twenty year drought on Nantucket. Several key starters from the previous Vineyard team were back, including starting QB Jason Dyer, wide receivers Albie Robinson and Jason O'Donnell, linebackers T.R. Fullin, Tom Woods, Sam Hayes, and Rusty Ventura, along with several other three year starters.

It is important to mention that in 1988, both my first year at MV and my first time playing on Nantucket, the MV Touchdown Club chartered a fan boat to Nantucket. That was a first. The football team would fly to Nantucket but take the fan boat home, while several hundred fans would make the four hour, round trip boat ride. Several chartered flights were also available for fans. All in all, in attendance that day in November were several thousand fans from both islands. I would commonly joke, "If you were a thief, the best time to break into someone's house would be on the day of the Island Cup game, for most islanders would be at the game."

The Martha's Vineyard-Nantucket game is a big event for the host school. The day's festivities began at 10:00 a.m. when the junior varsity game starts. The main event, the varsity game, started at 1:00 p.m.

The 1992 varsity game started off as expected with both teams showing emotional and intense play. Nantucket took an early lead on a one yard run by Aaron Fox. Nantucket's two-point conversion attempt failed. With the Vineyard struggling to move the football, due to a well-designed and executed defensive game plan, Nantucket eventually took a 12-0 lead with just 4:41 left to play in the game. As the Vineyard offense was preparing to take the field, I gathered the team around me and said, "Men, if you think the game is over, then it is."

We took the field knowing that our passing game was going to have to start being successful. I made a simple blocking adjustment that proved to be valuable. We would align with our trips formation (three receivers to one side of the ball) and keep the near slot in to block. That gave us two blockers on the perimeter for our sprint-out game. Before this adjustment, Nantucket had been able to outnumber our blocking on our sprint-outs, bringing one more defender than we had blockers. The result was several QB sacks or errant passes.

The Vineyard faced a crucial third down play. I called a sprint-out to our right. The near slot made his block allowing Jason Dyer, QB, to get onto the perimeter and get a clear view downfield. He hit our senior receiver, Jason O'Donnell, who made a great over-the-shoulder catch, for a significant gain.

With time ticking away, under four minutes left, we ran one of our better combination routes that had the middle slot running a simple out route and our wide receiver, Albie Robinson, running a chair route, a simple out-and-up route. Again, Jason Dyer rolled out to his right, but this time the FB did not secure his block on the blitzing middle linebacker. Dyer had to pull up short. As Dyer was being pulled down by his jersey, he was able to get enough on the throw to hit Albie Robinson who was streaking down the sideline, executing his chair route.

With the ball in the air, Albie made a diving catch, catching the ball in the back corner of the end zone with his fingertips, the Vineyard's first points of the day. This play would later be referred to in Vineyard football lore as, "The Catch," and is regarded to be one of the biggest plays in Vineyard football history. Junior FB/DE Mike Dowd came on and kicked the extra point, Nantucket 12 Vineyard 7.

Our ensuing kickoff was a deep squib kick that was almost recovered by Vineyarder Howie Ditson. The defense stiffened and forced a three and out. Covering the punt, Nantucket tackled returner Jason Dyer out-of-bounds on our sideline. That gave us the left side as the wide side of the field. Once again the offense aligned in our trips formation to the wide side, our left, with our speedy and physical Keith Devine as the wide receiver. We ran our combination route to the left with the middle receiver running a corner route and the outside receiver running an out route. The QB read the coverage and threw the football to Keith, the receiver running the out.

Keith caught the ball, turned upfield, broke an arm tackle, and raced fifty yards for the go ahead touchdown. Dan Borer, the middle receiver who had run the corner route, had turned back once Keith had caught the pass and made a block that took out two would-be Nantucket defenders. Mike Dowd kicked his second extra point giving the Vineyard a 14-12 lead.

Why not go for two points to take a three point lead? That was a question often asked of me. My response has always been the same, "We had momentum, why do something to take it away? They didn't have a kicking game and wouldn't be attempting a field goal."

With under a minute to play and the Vineyard up 14-12, our defense was called upon once again to make a huge stop. We again kicked a deep squib kick and looked to be in great shape to win the game. Then, we almost made a crucial mistake. If not for the outstanding, individual effort by sophomore, two-way starter Aaron Belanger, DT-OT, Nantucket would have taken the lead and probably won the game. On a crucial third down play, Nantucket ran a double pass, a similar play they used in the first half with success.

The original play had their talented tailback, Aaron Fox, aligned deep in the I-formation. On the snap of the ball, he ran a swing pass out of the backfield to his right. The QB, Dennis Caron, looked off the deep defenders and threw a flair pass to Aaron. Aaron caught the ball and gained significant yardage. At half-time Vineyard outside linebacker, Rusty Ventura, told me that he had diagnosed that play. He was ready if Nantucket decided to run it again.

Nantucket did run it again and Rusty was ready. However, this time the pass was a lateral thrown toward the Nantucket bench. Rusty was able to knock the pass down. With the ball on the ground and no whistle yet blown, our entire coaching staff was screaming for our defense to get on the ball, for it was now considered a fumble. A Nantucket player, none other than Aaron Fox (who had already scored both of the Nantucket touchdowns), picked up the ball and started running down their sideline. Aaron Belanger saw the play happening from the other side of the field. He executed the pursuit drill to perfection making a diving, shoestring tackle. Aaron Fox was knocked down on the Vineyard twenty five yard line with time enough for just one more play.

The Vineyard used its "Victory Defense." That brought Jason Dyer into the game as a deep safety, standing in the end zone behind our regular safety, Albie Robinson. Dennis Caron, who had played an outstanding game, dropped back and threw a Hail Mary down the middle of the field. Jason Dyer went up and made the game-clinching interception at the Vineyard five yard line. Game over.

Martha's Vineyard had won in dramatic style, overcoming a 12-0 deficit with just 4:41 left in the game. It was the first win for Martha's Vineyard on Nantucket in twenty years.

As the final second ticked off the clock, Vineyard fans flooded the game field. There were lots of hugs, kisses, and congratulations all around. The Vineyard had defended its title and was able to keep the cup for the second consecutive year, the third MV Island Cup win in five years.

After the team had packed up its belongings in the locker room, there were two Nantucket school buses ready outside the gym. The junior varsity and their coaches were on one bus and the varsity and coaches on the second. I was the last person to step on the bus.

Just as I was ready to sit down, Dennis Caron, Nantucket's senior QB stepped onto the bus. All the yelling and celebrating stopped, and you could now hear a pin drop. Much to my surprise and to the surprise of all on that bus, Dennis asked me if he could address our team. Not sure what to expect, I said, "Yes."

You could tell that only forty-five to sixty minutes or so removed from the game, Dennis was still emotional. He stood on our bus and faced our team. He congratulated the Vineyard players, coaches and fans on playing a fantastic game and wished us good luck in the upcoming Super Bowl. Our players responded with a standing ovation and a team, "Thank you."

To this day, I am still in awe of what Dennis did that day. Here was this seventeen or eighteen-year-old high school athlete who had just lost his last high school football game at home. That loss cost his team a League Championship and possible Super Bowl win. The character and integrity Dennis demonstrated were incredible. Dennis showed just how much class he had. I hope his family is as proud of him as I was that day.

Sports and competition teach a person many life lessons. Dennis taught me something that day. That lesson was to play the game hard, respect your opponent, and always show class, win or lose. Outside of football I did not know Dennis, but I would be surprised if he hasn't been successful in his life's journey.

Upon our arrival back onto Martha's Vineyard, the football team was met by what seemed to be the entire island population. The team and all its members were the last to walk off the boat's freight deck. As we walked off the boat, there were police, fire, and ambulance lights flashing and sirens blaring. It was a welcome home like I have never experienced.

To this day, that reception is one of my fondest memories of coaching on Martha's Vineyard. Fortunately, we have repeated that welcome numerous times, but there is something special about the first one.

CHAPTER 8

"Remaining childish is a tremendous state of innocence." - John Lydon

Being a career high school football coach, I have always believed in running a disciplined program, a program that was respected and one in which students enjoyed being a participant. With that said, I had set policies in place for my program. One of those was our travel policy.

When playing games away from the Vineyard, there was a progression of activities. These started with our athletes arrival at the Steamship Authority terminal, SSA, in either Vineyard Haven or Oak Bluffs, two towns on Martha's Vineyard. Players were to come thirty minutes before their forty-five minute ferry ride to Woods Hole.

Once in America (as we islanders call the mainland), the team boarded a school bus that stayed parked in one of the Steamship Authority parking lots. The team then made the long, school bus ride to the opponent's field. When the game was over, the team boarded the bus which returned to Woods Hole, and awaited the next forty-five minute ferry boat ride back to Martha's Vineyard. All in all, including the boat, bus, and game time, an away football game involved an average of about nine hours. On any away game, several things could go wrong.

When the football team traveled, each player and coach had to dress according to the team dress code which involved wearing a collared, button-down dress shirt, a tie, dress pants with belt, socks, and dress shoes.

No hats were allowed. Violators of any of the above stipulations would not be allowed to travel. The dress code also applied to return trips. When adults saw our team dressed up, they commonly made positive comments about how nice the young men looked. That, in itself, helped promote our sport and our school.

Back in 1994, after practice one Friday, I reminded the junior varsity and varsity to be at the SSA at 8:00, thirty minutes before the 8:30 a.m. boat departure time. I also reminded them to come appropriately dressed for the game. Of course, that meant to come dressed as described above.

The next morning, Ben Higgins, a freshman on his first away game, took me literally. He showed up at the boat dressed in his game pants, game socks, jersey and cleats along with the rest of his gear in the issued equipment bag. The coaches and other players said nothing to him before I arrived. They wanted to see and hear my reaction. I can't remember my exact words or facial expression, but it must have been special. I asked the young player what he was doing coming to the boat dressed like that? His response was simple enough, "Coach, you told us to come dressed for the game." Having no suitable retort, I made a one-time exception to my travel policy. The freshman was allowed to travel and play that day.

Ben, who became a four-year varsity player at running back, earned the nickname Bambi. There were numerous times Ben would be bent in half when tackled. When this happened, he simply stood up, shook his shoulders, kicked one leg out at a time, and jogged back to the huddle. The scene was reminiscent of young Bambi sliding around on the ice before getting his footing.

You would not have known it from his inauspicious beginning, but this young man would go on to excel in both football and track and field. As a junior Ben would finish ninth in the nation in the long jump and would earn a partial track scholarship to the University of Florida. In 1997, his senior year, Ben became the school's single-season rushing record holder. That year would be our first undefeated season and the school's third Super Bowl Championship in three attempts.

CHAPTER 9

"I never learn anything talking. I only learn things by asking questions." - *Lou Holtz*

Martha's Vineyard Regional High School (MVRHS) has an excellent track record and reputation for placing its graduates at some of the top colleges and universities across the United States, which happens on a yearly basis.

It has been said that an education at MVRHS is like obtaining a private school education at a public school cost. Of course, not all graduates go on to college. Several go to trade schools, go into the Armed Forces, or find jobs on MV right out of high school. The bottom line is that graduates from MVRHS are well prepared for life beyond high school.

Our students get exposed to a wide variety of opportunities, but not all of our students take full advantage of them. For some, sports, specifically football, provide the motivation to stay in school, pass their classes, and graduate. For these students, sports is their way of being recognized. People often told me, "If not for football, (player's name) would not have graduated."

We had one such player on the 1994 football team. I would like to tell a story about Richard Travis (not his real name). Richard was a senior that year. He had a mother who loved him but no father in the home, and he was an only child. Richard was outgoing and loyal but struggled academically. He had a wild spirit and some said that he was obnoxious. As with many of my players, I gave him an endearing nickname reflecting some of the unfortunate things that happened to him, but he was a tough kid and took it in good humor.

Early in the 1994 season, we had an away game. I had suspended the starting fullback for that game for skipping the last practice of the week, and he didn't even make the trip. On the ride to the game my second string fullback, Dan Broderick, injured his neck on the bus. Precisely what happened, I don't know. All I do know is that Dan could not move his head. We tried a hot shower, massage, and Tylenol. Nothing worked to relieve his discomfort. Once we arrived at the field, I had to teach Richard the plays at the fullback position. Having Richard playing fullback forced me to narrow down our offensive play selection. Even though we lost the game, Richard did an admirable job that day. His efforts earned him more playing time at fullback for the rest of the season.

A new tradition I started at MV was Homecoming. Before my arrival, the Vineyard had never had a homecoming game. In fact, I asked my interview committee, "Who does the Vineyard traditionally play for Homecoming?" Their response was, "What is Homecoming?" That was the first clue that I had a lot of work to do here.

Back in Georgia, next to the rival game, homecoming week and the homecoming game are the most significant events of the football season, if not the entire school year. Homecoming is the welcoming back of alumni, on one specific weekend, during the football season. The students and faculty enthusiastically decorated the high school and the students participated in a car parade. There was the crowning of the homecoming queen and king, who were students from the senior class and a festive homecoming dance that followed the game. Homecoming was a big deal.

Fast forward to the middle of the 1994 season. Homecoming week was approaching.

We were having a team meeting in one of the school's classrooms. Having just finished showing the game film from the week before, as I was standing in front of the team about to start discussing our next opponent, Richard raised his hand. When I called on him, innocently, he asked, "Coach Herman, is this year's homecoming game going to be home or away?"

I didn't know what to say. I was at a loss. Players and coaches looked around at each other in utter amazement. I always believed that there was no such thing as a stupid question. However, when Richard asked if Homecoming was going to be home or away, I was forced to reconsider my position.

Once I got over the shock of the question, I looked directly at Richard and asked him, "What part of home...coming don't you understand?" I honestly think the rest of the team was laughing too hard to hear my answer. Without giving Richard another chance to sound foolish, I replied, "Yes, Richard. This year's homecoming game will be home." Surprisingly, I would have that same question asked again in my last year of coaching. This time I was better prepared to answer. I responded with, "Hey, dumb-smart kid, it's called homecoming for a reason. Get it now?"

Embarrassed, the player answered simply, "Yes, coach."

Another of Richard's interesting questions comes to mind. Again, we were in a classroom environment. The team had finished watching the previous week's game film. Richard raised his hand and I called on him. This time he asked, "Coach, are we going to play any home night games this year?" Now, you might be thinking that question had plenty of merit. However, back in 1994, the Vineyard did not have lights at the game field. We would not have lights installed until August of 1999.

Once again, my no stupid question position came back to mind. I always felt that if one person asked a question, there must be someone else who wanted to know the answer but was afraid to ask. However, I had a hard time believing someone else was thinking the same things as Richard.

Of course, the entire team was again laughing at Richard for asking such a bizarre question. But, not to belittle Richard, I calmly asked him, "Do you see any light poles or lights at the game field?"

Richard innocently answered, "No coach. So, no home night games?"

I responded, "You're a quick learner. Now, you are answering your own questions."

As if that wasn't enough from Richard, there was more still to come. However, this time it would not come in the form of a question. Instead, it would be in his action.

The 1994 team played its last game of the year at Nantucket. In the first quarter of the game, Richard scored the game's first points, putting the

Vineyard ahead 6-0. Richard was celebrating his touchdown by running toward our bench. He was holding up two fingers as if to say, "We're number two." Most players in that same situation would hold up one finger, symbolizing we're number one. A photographer from the Martha's Vineyard Times captured Richard's celebration sign. That photo was on the front page of the paper that next week. FYI, we lost the game to Nantucket.

I wish I could tell you that Richard was the last of my players to ask questions that were dumbfounding, but I would be lying. It just so happens that the question, "Is the homecoming game home or away?" was the first and only question that left me speechless. No other question even came close. After graduation Richard went on to start his own landscaping business.

MVRHS continued the tradition of having a homecoming game. We made that week special. A king and queen were crowned, along with a prince and princess from each grade, which makes up the homecoming court. The winners are announced, then crowned, at the homecoming dance.

And yes, Homecoming is always a home game.

CHAPTER 10

"My wallet is like an onion, opening it makes me cry." - Anonymous

I have a reputation for being cheap, but I consider myself thrifty. My staff and I would frequently eat out together, and I never offered nor had the money needed to cover the entire bill. Sometimes I barely had enough to cover my own meal. However, one night after a coaches' clinic, my coaches and I ate dinner together. When the bill came, I took out my wallet and made a $5 contribution toward the tip. One of my assistants was shocked. He said, "Oh my God. You actually have money in that wallet." At our next seasons end-of-the-year banquet, that same coach presented me with a gift. He had taken the $5 bill I had left as the tip and put it inside a picture frame. He gave me the frame with the money inside. Naturally, after a few days, I broke into the frame and took back my $5.

Every year my coaching staff attended at least one football coaching clinic, sometimes more. We did this to stay up-to-date with any new techniques and schemes. Moreover, this allowed us the opportunity to bond, away from the day-to-day grind of our sport. We often attended The Big New England Football Clinic held in Newport, Rhode Island. This clinic usually took place the first or second weekend in March and ran from Thursday afternoon through Saturday night. The MV Touchdown Club (our football booster club) covered the cost for us to attend. The Touchdown Club generously paid for the three or four hotel rooms we reserved. They also covered our clinic registration fee. The school provided transportation in the form of a twelve passenger van.

Nantucket also attended this clinic. Their football coach, Vito Capizzo, and I made arrangements to travel together. His staff met us at a local restaurant at the Bourne Bridge in Bourne, Massachusetts. Their staff rode to the clinic in the van along with mine. Driving and attending the clinic together allowed our two staffs the opportunity of getting to know each other on a more personal level. One year in particular was a little more eventful than the others.

The hotel where we were staying had just completed a major renovation. As we were registering, Vito realized the receptionist had been one of his past students. You may be able to tell from his name that Vito is Italian. Vito, like many Italians, enjoyed wine, red wine to be more precise. As Vito reached into his pocket to take out his credit card, he dropped the brown paper bag that he was holding. The bag hit the lightly carpeted floor hard and made a loud sound. The contents of the container broke. In a matter of seconds, the newly replaced carpet began to turn dark red. Inside the bag was an expensive bottle of red wine that Vito planned on enjoying. The entire bottle spilled onto the carpet. That was just the start of happenings that weekend. Embarrassed, Vito said, "Timeout, I fumbled." He apologized to his former student. The rest of us just laughed.

The clinic weekend went as usual. The Nantucket staff and my staff attended some of the same sessions together. We found ourselves attending sessions in the hopes of trying to learn how to beat each other. On Saturday morning we had plans to leave the clinic around noon to get home on one of the later ferries that night. Three of my assistants and I were enjoying a buffet breakfast in the hotel. When our waitress brought me the bill, I asked her, "Can I charge the breakfast to my hotel room?" After she said yes, I gave her the room number, and we left for clinic sessions and then home.

Two months later I ran into Vito. He called me over to where he was standing. He said, "Hey Snake (his pet name for me), I got my credit card bill last month, and there was a $90 charge for breakfast from the clinic hotel on it. What the hell was that?"

I simply told him, "Thank you for breakfast. I charged our coaches' breakfasts to your hotel room. That's what you get for beating us last year." Of course, he let out a few Italian expressions and said, "We're gonna kick your ass again next year too." We both had a good laugh, and actually, Nantucket did beat us again that next year. From that point on, Vito was more guarded with his credit card around me.

Vito and I were good friends. I vividly remember the first time we met. I came to the Vineyard in June of 1988 to meet with prospective players. While I was on Martha's Vineyard, the Cape and Islands Athletic Directors were holding their end–of–the–year AD's meeting at Farm Neck Golf Club on the Vineyard. The Martha's Vineyard Regional High School played most of their sports in the Cape and Islands League. The AD's invited me to have lunch with them. As I walked up to Farm Neck, they asked me if I had met Vito yet. I responded, "What's a Vito?" It didn't take me long to discover just exactly what a Vito was. The Vineyard AD, Anne Lemenager, introduced me to Vito as Donald, the name I preferred being called.

Vito approached me, shook my hand and said, "Donnie, welcome to the Vineyard." He is the only person I have ever allowed to call me Donnie.

Once I became the Athletic Director at MVRHS from 1990-1994, Vito and I spent a lot of time together away from football. It was during these years that I got to know Vito as the man he was. From 1988 through the fall of 2008, Vito and I competed against each other on the football field. Many of those games were legendary. While we were rivals one day a year, we were good friends the rest of the year. I have no doubt that our rivalry made both of us better coaches. Playing each other brought out the best in both of us. Sadly, on May 17th, 2018, Vito passed away at the age of 78.

Long after our coaching careers have come to an end, I still have the utmost respect for Vito; what he did as a football coach, as a mentor to thousands, and for helping put Nantucket on the map. His Hall of Fame legend and legacy will live on as the high school football stadium on Nantucket was named the "Vito Capizzo Stadium" in 2009.

CHAPTER 11

"Most football players are temperamental. That's 90% temper and 10% mental." -
Doug Plank

Unquestionably, certain players leave their mark on the program from their performance on the field. Some leave theirs in other ways. Fred Noyes left his mark on our program from his off-season efforts and his on-field performance.

I gave Fred the nickname of Bamm-Bamm from the Flintstones' cartoon character. Fred was a strong young man but didn't know just how strong he was. He relied more on his strength than his athleticism. Fred was involved in our program for five years, because he was allowed to play on our junior varsity team as an eighth grader. His parents, Cheryl and Al, were actively involved in the MV Touchdown Club those same years. They were supportive and visible people around our program. For two years Fred started at defensive tackle on the varsity team and occasionally played as a backup offensive lineman.

The morning of our last regular season game against Nantucket, Fred's junior year, he asked me if he could switch game jersey numbers. Usually he wore number 55. He asked if he could wear number 95 just this one time. Fred never told me why he wanted to change numbers. I allowed him to do so, reasoning I did not anticipate him playing offensive line in this game.

Fred had a solid performance, playing every snap on defense. We won the game, stayed undefeated, and were heading for the school's third Super Bowl. Plans had been made to hold a team victory celebration in the school cafeteria shortly after the game. I was the last person to arrive, because I had postgame coaching duties to attend. As I walked in, I looked over and saw that Fred's mom was crying. I went over to her and asked, "Why are you crying?" She answered, "I didn't see my son play today."

I asked, "Why not, where were you?"

She replied, "I watched the entire game but never saw Freddie play. I didn't see number 55 on defense the entire game."

Fighting back my reaction, I said to Cheryl, "Fred wore number 95 today. He asked me if he could switch jerseys for this game. Didn't Fred tell you? He played every snap on defense and played great. You mean to tell me after all these years of watching your son play, you don't know what his running form looks like?"

Cheryl looked at me in amazement and started crying all over again. This time she was crying tears of embarrassment.

That happened in 1997. We went on to win our third Super Bowl title. Fred wore his usual number fifty-five. His Mom saw him play every defensive snap in our Super Bowl win over Westwood High School.

Later, when Fred was a senior in 1998, we were once again playing Nantucket but this time on Nantucket. We would not qualify for the postseason, so this would be our last game. Fred was a captain. We had a specific stretching routine. After our team stretch, the captains, who were standing in front of their rows, ran down their line, chest-bumped and high-fived all the players in their respective line. Once they got to the last man, they turned and sprinted back to the front of their line for our quick calisthenics. Also, as part of the team stretching routine, used only against Nantucket, I walked up to each player and whispered something personal to them.

We had done this routine for years. The players aligned themselves in the same lines for every practice and game. As our captains began running down their lines, Bamm-Bamm was excited. He approached one of our starting offensive tackles, Jack McGroarty. Instead of chest-bumping Jack, Fred impulsively gave him an unexpected head butt.

As our stretching phase ended, the team moved on to our remaining pregame routine. I looked over at our bench and saw our trainer working

45

on one of our players as the Nantucket team doctor was walking over as well. The player, who I still had not identified, was lying on his back. I walked over to the bench to find that Jack McGroarty was the injured player. Keep in mind, all we had done so far was stretch.

I asked Jack, "What's wrong?"

He calmly said, "Fred head-butted me."

The Nantucket doctor told me that Jack had whiplash as a result of the head butt and wouldn't be able to play. He then placed a neck collar on Jack.

I was dumbfounded. Bamm-Bamm played in our program for five years. He worked so hard to become the player he was. Surprisingly though, nobody was shocked when I told the team and coaches that Jack had whiplash as a result of Fred's headbutt.

Our team and Fred played inspired football that afternoon; however Nantucket beat us that day. After this accidental injury, I disallowed any future headbutts.

CHAPTER 12

"Your talent determines what you can do. Your motivation determines how much you are willing to do. Your attitude determines how well you do it." - Lou Holtz

Players develop and mature at different times. It is not uncommon for athletes to excel on the game field but have issues in their everyday life. The problem I am referring to here is behavior.

Two of the ultimate homer announcers, Ken Goldberg and the late Norm Vunk, gave players nicknames. One such player was Teddy Bennett, and his nickname was Teddy Ballgame.

Teddy excelled during his senior year and became a Mayflower League All-Star linebacker and running back. However, Teddy was a little on the wild side. Before his senior year, he would frequently get into trouble at school and brought negative attention to the football program. It was so bad that I placed Teddy on an out-of-season behavior contract. He was one screw up away from not playing his senior year. Both he and his father signed the contract.

It was now the start of the 1999 season. We used to conduct a conditioning test on the first day of practice. One phase of this test was a two mile run. Players had to complete the run in a predetermined time based on their size and offensive position. Failure to finish in the specified time placed the athlete in the breakfast club.

The breakfast club meant that the player had to show up thirty minutes early to the next day's first session and run two miles. That meant a 6:00

a.m. start time for our 6:30 a.m. practice. Players continued to run the two miles each morning until making their time or until the double sessions were over.

During the 1999 conditioning test, I passed out tongue depressors for the coaches to give to the players at the half way point. The players would have to hand the tongue depressors in as they crossed the finish line. As predicted, Teddy did not make his time, along with several other players. They all qualified for the breakfast club the next day.

That night, after the first practice, I wrote numbers on every tongue depressor. The same procedure took place that second morning. Keep in mind that all tongue depressors were blank on day one but they all had numbers on day two. I was standing at the finish line of the two mile run and as I looked up I saw Teddy sprinting down the final stretch. It looked like he was going to make his time. As the players approached I started calling out split times. Teddy crossed the finish line well ahead of his qualifying time. As Teddy crossed the finish line, he handed me his tongue depressor. I called out the time and announced that Teddy qualified. I then looked at the tongue depressor to find it was blank. I asked Teddy, "Why isn't there a number on this tongue depressor?"

Teddy just smiled and said, "Coach, you caught me. I'll see you tomorrow morning for the breakfast club."

At the midseason mark, our team was undefeated and playing well. It was early in the school day on a Wednesday. I walked down the hall and saw Teddy walking ahead of me going around the corner. He did not see me. I overheard a female friend of Teddy invite him to a party that upcoming weekend. Teddy stopped and told the girl, "Thanks for the invite, but I have to be on my best behavior for the next three months. I won't be there."

I thought to myself, "Wow, this kid is maturing and trying to become a team leader." Of course, I never let Teddy know that I heard this conversation. As I stated earlier, Teddy matured right in front of me.

The 1999 team finished 11-0, our second undefeated season in three years, and won the school's fourth Super Bowl title. Teddy was one of the main reasons for the team's success. Interestingly enough, Tom Bennett and Teddy Bennett are the only father-son duo to go undefeated while playing football at MVRHS. In 1963, Tom Bennett's senior year, his team went 6-0-1. Teddy was able to one-up his father by having a perfect season in his senior year.

Over the years Teddy and I have remained in contact with each other. He often reminds me of the valuable lessons he learned while playing for me; lessons he still applies in his everyday life. Hearing those expressions of appreciation are priceless to me. Here is an example of one such letter:

"I am very pleased to know you recognized the change that began in me, as I grew mentally and emotionally - from a boy towards becoming a man in that last season. Without the accountability, camaraderie, discipline, and passion the TEAM provided me, I would not have been afforded the lessons that your leadership and our program taught me. At the time you presented me with that contract I was very displeased by the position I found myself in. The problem for me internally was that, I knew I had put myself into that position being a young man very much driven by dissent, questioning of authority and establishment ideas.

I, as so many young men, was incredibly sensitive but feelings manifested in ways that got me into trouble. This "out of season contract" was the spear point of my personal growth in so many ways coach. My behavior had to adjust if I was going to remain a part of my team. Not only would I be devastated to not play the game I love most - and at the pinnacle of my football life that began when I was 7 years old - but more importantly, I would be letting down my family and friends. I had managed to talk, play, and fight my way out of just about everything until this point.

This is where I began hearing your words in repetition: discipline, accountability, overcoming adversity, dig deep ... TEAM/me ... even the word gentlemen. I utilized these words and ideas as fuel to become outstanding and to prove everyone wrong (again in defiance) but now with the purpose of showing all the people who took the extra time and effort to push me and to realize my potential. I still live by these words and repeat them to people every chance I get because these are some of the most valuable lessons I've learned even to this day."

CHAPTER 13

"Strength does not come from winning. Your struggles develop your strengths. When you go through hardships and decide not to surrender, that is strength." – Arnold Schwarzenegger

When you live on Martha's Vineyard, you learn that there are certain people who Islanders consider family. Such was the case with Richie Madeiras.

Richie Madeiras was born on Martha's Vineyard on November 24, 1954, making him a native islander. He attended Martha's Vineyard Regional High School and graduated in 1973. While in high school, Richie played four years of football. He later married Sue Ciampa in 1983. They lived in Oak Bluffs, one of the six towns that make up the Vineyard. Richie became the Oak Bluffs Shellfish Warden and he and Sue had two children, daughter Elyse and son Ben.

Ben and my middle child, Adam, were the same age and attended the Oak Bluffs Elementary School together. They played on several youth sports teams, both with and against each other. The number one sport they played together was travel soccer.

In addition to my coaching job at the high school, I tried to coach my own kids in as many youth sports as I could. This was the case with youth basketball and Little League baseball. I first coached an all-star Little League baseball team when Ben and Adam were in the third grade. I continued coaching their all-star baseball teams through their Little League years. I traveled with their soccer team, as a spectator, as often as my schedule would allow. Richie, Ben's dad, also traveled. It was during these times that Richie and I began our friendship.

Many people have said that Richie and I could have been related. We both had similar builds, similar skin tones, and dark hair. Richie sported a beard, while I had a mustache. People said our personalities were similar. Richie was a good guy, so I took that as a compliment.

Life and football were both going well in 1999. At the middle of the 1999 football season our team was undefeated.

On a typically normal Tuesday in October, we were on the practice field preparing for our upcoming away game to be played that Saturday. Around 4:00 p.m., the mother of one of our players came to the practice field to give her son the news that Richie was missing. I allowed that player to leave practice to be with his family, not quite knowing what was really happening.

When I got home for dinner that night, I heard that Richie had been out fishing on his boat. His boat was seen floating offshore, but Richie was nowhere to be found.

Bad news travels fast on Martha's Vineyard. It was shortly after the news that his boat was seen floating, that a search and rescue party was sent out looking for Richie. As darkness settled in that Tuesday night, so did the reality that Richie might have drowned.

To support his family, I went to the Madeiras' home. The thought was that Richie must have drowned. His body, however, was still missing.

Ben, then in the fifth grade, and Elyse, a ninth grader at the high school, were distraught. Sue seemed to be in shock and was trying hard to maintain some semblance of composure for her children.

The next day came and went with no update. The mood at the high school and with our team was somber. We continued with our daily lives the best we could, but our thoughts and prayers were with the Madeiras family.

Two days later the reality was confirmed. Richie's body was found tangled in seaweed just offshore from where his boat was found. The common thought was that he fell overboard. While Richie was wearing his waders, he was not wearing a life vest. Apparently, his waders filled up with water and pulled him down.

I was trying to think of a way to honor Richie and at the same time honor his family. The weekend after Richie's funeral would be the football team's first home game since his passing.

The idea came to me to have Elyse and Ben serve as honorary captains for the Blue Hills game, an important league game.

Earlier, I mentioned Richie played football for the high school. When he was a junior, Martha's Vineyard played a football game at Blue Hills in Canton, Massachusetts. Richie suffered a critical, season-ending injury during that game and was airlifted to a Boston hospital. Jay Schofield, the high school's athletic director, was at the game. Jay stayed with Richie when the team returned for the ferry home. Richie lacerated his liver, which called for half of it to be removed. I was unaware that the liver is one of the few organs that is capable of growing back. Such was the case with Richie.

Richie was cleared to return to football for his senior year and he was named a team captain.

What better team to play against with his children as honorary captains than Blue Hills? Both squads were undefeated. Blue Hills had the division's leading rusher on their team.

Despite the game being played on Martha's Vineyard, the *Boston Globe* picked Blue Hills and predicted, "Blue Hills will part the Vineyard Sound on their way to an easy victory." My players were already excited about playing this game. They knew the importance of this game, not only for league ramifications, but also for the Madeiras family. The statement in the *Boston Globe* just threw kerosene on an already burning fire.

Blue Hills ran an effective wing-T offense and had a running back that made it work. Anticipating the importance of this game, I had researched defenses that were effective against the wing-T. Martha's Vineyard used an even-front defense ever since I arrived there in 1988. I knew that if we did something out of the ordinary, we could confuse them.

Scouring the internet, I found a wide 7 defense. I studied that defense and its installation and felt that we had the personnel to run that defense.

During the week of practice, our coaches did an excellent job of preparing our team. Our players really bought into running the wide 7 and were excited to see it in action.

The night we played was about as perfect as a football night could be.

The wind was mild, unusual for the Vineyard field. The temperature was in the comfortable mid 50s. There wasn't a cloud in the sky and there was a full moon.

That wide 7 defense could not have worked any better. Blue Hills would not get a first down until late in the second quarter. Their good back ran off a forty yard run down to our fifteen yard line, but that was the closest to our goal line they were able to reach all night. Along with our defense playing outstandingly, our offense was also running on all cylinders.

With roughly three minutes left in the game, we scored our last touchdown, making the score 33-0. We aligned in our special extra point formation, the swinging gate. My holder called the team in so that we would kick the extra point. We got a bad snap from the center. One of the special team plays we practice is a bad snap on extra points. We have a set play, called fire. The holder yells out, "Fire!" and we execute a pass play.

This was exactly what happened on that bad snap. We executed the fire play to perfection. The holder, backup QB Kyle Crossland, made a nice throw to an open receiver in the back of the end zone. The score was 35-0, which was the final score.

When the game ended and both teams were lined up to shake hands, Elyse and Ben were also in line. As we were walking down the line, someone told me to look at the scoreboard. I looked over and saw the full moon in the background with the 35-0 score still lit up. I said, "Wow, the moon looks nice."

That person said, "No, coach. Look at the score. Richie wore #35 as a player."

I still get chills when I think about that final score.

After shaking hands, our team traditionally performed a winning ritual only done at home. They made a large circle at the thirty yard line. One player stood in the middle holding the game ball. The player threw the ball high in the air and as the ball hit the ground, all players fell on their backs.

After the Blue Hills game, the players selected Ben to be the person to throw the ball in the air. After the ritual ended, the players picked Ben up and carried him off the field on their shoulders. Elyse was behind the team bench standing with her mother and friends. Many of the fans were still in the stands watching this ritual.

The Madeiras family appreciated the way the football team chose to honor Richie and his family. We always preached that if someone plays football for the Vineyard, that person belongs to the Vineyard football family.

That family grows each year. At the conclusion of the 1999 season, we established the Richie Madeiras Captain's Award. Each captain receives a Richie Madeiras Captain's plaque. Also, there is the Richie Madeiras Captain's Memorial plaque which has the names of the captains engraved on a plate. This memorial plaque stays on display near the high school trophy case.

What better way for our football family to honor a football family member from years ago.

CHAPTER 14

"In times like these, it is good to remember that there have always been times like these." - Paul Harvey

During most of my coaching career on Martha's Vineyard, the players and coaches flew on the Saturday prior to Thanksgiving for the games against Nantucket. Cape Air, a local airline based in Hyannis, Massachusetts on Cape Cod, provided several nine passenger planes. The flight took ten to fifteen minutes. Our fans, cheerleaders, and the junior high football team traveled to the game on a chartered Steamship Authority (SSA) boat. Ticket sales and fundraisers paid for the boat.

I was in charge of creating the seating list for the flights which began departing the Vineyard at 7:30 a.m. Our junior varsity team was the first group to fly out, as they had a 10:00 kick off. Once they were all gone, our varsity would begin departing.

The year was 2002. I planned on going over early with the junior varsity team. My son, Adam, was playing on the junior high football team as an eighth grader. His kickoff time was the same as the junior varsity game and I wanted to watch him play.

The first couple of planes left without a problem. It took longer than usual for one plane to return after dropping off its first load. One of the aircraft had a flat tire on landing. That was not something someone who doesn't like flying wanted to hear.

Finally, the next three flights took off from MV. On my plane were eight freshman and sophomore football players including offensive lineman, Gustavo "Goose" Simoes. Goose tipped the scales at roughly 300 pounds.

As we began our takeoff, I noticed the wind was extreme and gusting. This flight made me think of how a roller coaster ride in the sky would feel. Several times the plane would hit a wind pocket, drop several feet, then rise again. While most of us were very nervous about the plane ride, Goose was having a blast. I heard him yell out, "Yahoo, this is great!" He was the only one on the plane with that sentiment.

Those ten minutes took forever. As we began our approach to the landing strip on Nantucket, once again we hit some turbulence. The pilot turned the nose of the plane perpendicular to the direction of the runway. I was seated in the copilot seat and my head was completely turned to the left looking at the landing strip. With twenty yards or so before touching down, the pilot turned the nose of the plane and made a safe landing.

As he touched down, I yelled out, "What the hell was that?"

The pilot said, "That type of landing, called crabbing, is commonly done in high winds."

I responded, "You think you could have told me ahead of time that you were going to do that?"

He said, "I didn't have time to explain."

We landed safely. In fact, all the planes landed safely. As we were getting out and walking into the airport, one of my assistant coaches, David Rossi, walked up to us with a giant smile on his face.

Pointing to the bathrooms he said, "The changing rooms are over there." The joke was that most of us needed the bathroom after that flight. We were all shaken up, except for Gustavo. He wanted the flight to last longer.

We boarded the school bus to take us to Nantucket High School. Once we arrived at the school, I received information that all the remaining planes on the Vineyard were grounded due to the high winds.

My immediate thoughts were, "Okay. My junior varsity team is here. My varsity team is stuck on MV. The fan boat left the Vineyard over an hour ago. I have no way of getting my varsity team over here. We're screwed."

I could not fathom what the fan boat ride must have been like. The boat ride took two hours on a good day. My son was on that boat. I envisioned a boatload of people throwing up. Ironically, because of the wind direction, the boat ride was relatively smooth, and the boat actually arrived early.

Roughly an hour later, the planes were cleared for takeoff. The kickoff time was changed to accommodate the delay in travel, but at least I would have my varsity team.

I think the only reason those planes flew was to get my players to Nantucket. The winds did not calm down. In fact, our athletic director, Glen Fields, decided to stay on Martha's Vineyard instead of taking the airplane roller coaster ride. He was not alone.

NBC Sports covered the game. They were going to show highlights of the game during the halftime of the Notre Dame football game later that day. They had several cameras spread around the field. One such camera was on a crane behind one end zone. However, because of the high winds, that camera was not used.

It took five planes to get my varsity and coaching staff to Nantucket. Once they all arrived at the school, my coaches told me that James Rebello, a junior, kissed the ground when he got out of the plane. Zach Mahoney, another junior, was crying. And, Bubba Bergeron, a senior, was throwing up an hour before kickoff from motion sickness.

On a typical day the wind on both Nantucket and Martha's Vineyard was usually gusty. However, today was an exception. During the junior high and junior varsity games, we experienced every kind of weather. It rained, it sleeted, it snowed, and then the sun came out. The high winds were the only constant weather feature.

After the junior varsity game ended, the varsity teams began their respective pregame warmup routines. I had my specialist in our kicking game on the field. My long snapper was snapping the ball to the punter into the wind, but the ball never traveled the needed distance. The wind was so strong that the ball was being blown back toward the center. I made sure all my kickers, snappers, and return guys worked from both directions. They had to know the effect the wind would have on the ball.

Finally, we started the game. We scored first. Ben Gunn, our senior kicker, was attempting to kick the extra point. We were at the end of the field where the wind was blowing into the kicker's face. Ben got his kick off without any trouble. The ball was going right down the middle of the uprights. As the ball went up and just before it was to cross the crossbar, the wind blew the ball back. No good. Because of the wind, the ball never broke the plane of the crossbar. The Vineyard was ahead 6-0.

Sadly, Nantucket would win the game that day by less than six points. In the second quarter Zach Mahoney recovered a Nantucket fumble and returned it for a touchdown only to have it negated on a phantom penalty.

Our loss in the 2002 game was the last time Nantucket won the Island Cup before my retirement in June of 2016. Martha's Vineyard went on to enjoy a thirteen game Island Cup win streak from 2003-2015.

Whenever I hear people complaining about wind conditions, I immediately go back to that day in November. That was the day I thought we were all going to die in a nine seater plane ride to Nantucket. That was also the day that Gustavo "Goose" Simoes enjoyed the flight of his life.

CHAPTER 15

"When you've got something to prove, there's nothing greater than a challenge."
- Terry Bradshaw

Bastille, also known as "Bass," was a big, athletic, but goofy kid. He was a starter on our varsity as a sophomore. He played defensive tackle and some offensive line.

The year was 2004 and we were going to play on Nantucket for the Island Cup. We had beaten the Nantucket Whalers in 2003 and won our fifth Super Bowl but most of that team had graduated. The 2004 team was currently 4-6 but could salvage the season with a win over Nantucket.

The season was not going well. It was a tough, mentally draining year for me. We lost players to injuries, I had to remove three varsity players for team rule violations, and we just weren't as athletic compared to teams of the past.

The junior high and junior varsity games came to an end early that afternoon. We lost both of those games.

At Nantucket's game field, there is a cyclone fence behind the visitors team bench. There is a large gate for players and team personnel to walk through and an ever-present, large, water puddle along our sideline. This puddle was exactly where our team stood during the game. It always amazed me how often and how hard it rained the night before we played on Nantucket. Eventually, I learned that Nantucket, did, indeed, flood our team area the night before we were to play them.

I was on the game field as my players were going through the first phase of our pregame warmup. Our specialists consisting of kickers, holders, returners, and snappers were going through their routines. Just as I was ready to call the rest of the team to one end zone, where we went for pregame, my long-time assistant coach, Bill Belcher, walked up to me.

Bill said, "Donald, I have good news, and I have bad news. Which do you want to hear first?"

I responded, "Oh boy, it's been that kind of year. Go ahead and give me the bad news first."

Bill said, "Bass tried to jump the fence behind our bench. He got his cleat stuck, fell and dislocated his shoulder."

I said, "What the hell? If that's the bad news, what's the good news."

Bill told me, "Their team doctor thinks he can put his shoulder back into place. Bass might still be able to play."

Bass gave a valiant effort. He ran down on the opening kickoff and then ran right off the field. Bass did not return. In fact, he required shoulder surgery that off-season.

Now that Bass wasn't playing, our defense became even more susceptible that day.

Earlier in the week, after viewing Nantucket game film, I noticed a weakness in their punt protection. On Wednesday of the game week, we were working on our punt return. I stopped the period and installed a new punt block by putting senior, Mike Shea, on the return team to rush and block their punt. Mike was not generally on the punt return team. I even went as far as to proclaim, "Mike, you are going to block their punt and EJ (our adept field goal kicker) is going to kick the game winning field goal."

It was the fourth quarter of the Island Cup game. Nantucket led 20-18 with less than three minutes to play. Nantucket had a first down at their forty yard line. We had three time-outs available and were in a must stop defensive series. Their QB did us a huge favor. Nantucket ran a QB sweep toward our sideline. Instead of falling to his knees and staying inbounds, he ran out of bounds, stopping the clock. That move saved us a time out. I helped their QB up off the ground and told him, "Thank you. Good job."

The next two offensive plays resulted in a total of five yards gained. We used a time-out after each run to stop the clock. It was fourth down and five from the Nantucket forty-five yard line. There were less than two minutes in the game and we had just one more time-out. I expected Nantucket to go for the first down. They lined up ready to run an offensive play. We told our defense to be disciplined, anticipating Nantucket trying to draw us offside.

Nantucket attempted to do just that, but we didn't fall for it. Wisely, they called a time-out to avoid taking a penalty. They lined up in their punting formation. Mike Shea entered the game and we had our special punt block called. The snap was good, and as their punter took his regular steps to punt the ball, Mike got through their protection and blocked the punt. We recovered the ball on Nantucket's thirty yard line. The Vineyard had new life.

We immediately went into our two minute offense. Junior QB, Ryan Rossi, hit senior receiver, Ryan Mello, on two consecutive passes that allowed Mello to get out of bounds. These plays stopped the clock without us having to use our last time-out.

We had the ball on the Nantucket twenty yard line with about thirty seconds remaining. Knowing that we had that one time-out gave us the option of running the ball.

We executed one of our better running plays; the quick trap to our fullback. Kyle Robertson hit the hole and was tackled inside the Whaler ten yard line. I allowed the game clock to run down to five seconds before taking our last time out.

We were now set to win the game with EJ Sylvia's twenty-five yard field goal. But, before we could attempt the kick, Nantucket took their last three time-outs in an attempt to ice EJ.

With Nantucket finally out of time-outs, we executed the field goal attempt. The ball sailed down the middle of the uprights with plenty of distance to spare.

We all thought the game was over. When we looked at the game clock, it still had three seconds on it. I never understood how that last play took only two seconds. We now had to kick off to Nantucket. They ran one of our kickoffs back for a touchdown earlier in the game.

EJ kicked a deep squib kick that was picked up by a Nantucket player. He attempted to run towards his bench, but we swarmed him. He got tackled by a host of MV defenders including junior, Lucas Landers.

Once again, we all thought the game was over. Our entire bench began running onto the field in celebration. At the very last second, we saw the football thrown up into the air to another Nantucket running back, the same back that returned the kickoff for a touchdown earlier.

As quickly as our bench emptied, our team ran back off the field. Everyone got back to the sideline except for our water boy, ten year old, Brendan Maseda. He ran onto the field to retrieve the kicking tee.

The Nantucket player was running down our sideline. I went from feeling the joy of victory to feeling that we were about to suffer the agony of defeat.

As the Nantucket player approached the fifty yard line, the water boy was trying to run off the field. He stopped and stepped back. Somehow, Lucas Landers, one of the original tacklers, executed the pursuit drill to perfection. He was one of two Vineyarders left that made the final tackle. They tackled the Nantucket player near our thirty-five yard line.

We all looked around, expecting a possible penalty flag for having too many players on the field, but instead we saw the officials running off the game field. Game over.

The Vineyard came back. Mike Shea blocked their punt. EJ Sylvia kicked the game winning field goal. It happened just as I predicted it on Wednesday.

All Mike Shea was able to say was, "How the hell did you know that was going to happen? I can't believe you called that. How did you know that was going to happen?"

What I do know was that we started the day down three players for discipline issues. We then started the game off by losing one of our defensive starters to a non-football related injury. We made a great special teams play and then went on a last minute scoring drive. Next, we kicked a game winning field goal that should have run the clock out. Still, we almost lost the game.

This game will forever be known as the *water boy* game. There was a picture taken of that last play that appeared in the local papers. The photo shows the Nantucket player running down our sideline. The water boy was seen stopped a few yards to the left of the player. The picture clearly shows that the water boy had zero impact on the play. However, Nantucket will always take exception to that statement. They felt we should have had a penalty thrown against us and that they should have had one more play. Nevertheless, we will always argue that the original ball carrier was down before making the lateral to his teammate.

Such is a rivalry!

CHAPTER 16

"I could have been a Rhodes Scholar, except for my grades." - Duffy Daugherty

One of the fun things I wanted to do for my teams was to have them attend college football games. I wanted my players to experience some of the same things I did when I was in high school. During high school I would frequently attend the University of Georgia home football games. After my Friday night games, I would load my father's car with friends and drive the four and a half hours to Athens, Georgia. Once there, we would spend the night on the railroad tracks.

The railroad tracks were across the street from one of the end zones. If we arrived early enough, we could stake claim to our territory and have a free seat, with a great view to watch the Saturday afternoon game. From time to time a train would pass through and we would all have to move out of the way. This location was also situated at the end of the stadium where the visiting team's locker room area was located. When they arrived, those of us on the tracks would heckle the opposing players.

Sadly, a few years after I graduated from college in 1981, Sanford Stadium (Georgia's stadium) expanded and enclosed both end zones. No longer can you sit on the railroad tracks and see inside the stadium.

In 1999, with the addition of lights on our game field, the opportunity for my teams to attend college football games became a reality.

One of my assistant coaches, Mike McCarthy, graduated from MVRHS in the late 1960's. He went on to play college football at the University of Connecticut, UCONN, and later worked at E.O. Smith High School in Storrs, Connecticut where UCONN is located. Mike's father, Dan, was the high school's first head football coach and athletic director. The Vineyard game field, now known as the Dan McCarthy Field, was named after him. Due to Mike's ties to the Vineyard, he moved his family back to the Vineyard where his three sons played football on my teams.

Because of Mike's connections with E.O. Smith High School, we made arrangements to scrimmage them. In 2004 MV played host to E.O. Smith in a preseason scrimmage. Our players and coaches were host families for their players and coaches.

E.O. Smith hosted Martha's Vineyard for a preseason scrimmage in 2005. The scrimmage took place at 10:00 a.m. the morning of a home UCONN football game. The E.O. Smith Booster Club held a cookout for both teams. Afterward, the Vineyard team attended the UCONN vs the University of Buffalo football game. All went well. Both teams looked impressive in the scrimmage and both sides enjoyed the cookout.

Our school bus parked in the bus parking lot at the UCONN stadium. The weather could not have been nicer. It was a sunny, cloudless afternoon, with temperatures in the low 80's. We all walked through the tailgaters on the way to the stadium. That alone was an eye-opening experience for most players on our team.

UCONN plays their football games at Rentschler Field, which used to be an airport. The parking and tailgating areas are spacious, to say the least. As we walked through the numerous campers and parties with tapped kegs of beer, and the usual tailgating games everywhere, we kept a close watch on our kids. At one point a few players stopped and attempted to play frisbee with a group of college students. Our players were enjoying themselves trying to take in everything. They were experiencing sensory overload, especially when it came to seeing the college girls.

We arrived in the UCONN stadium in time to watch both teams conduct their pregame warm ups. Even though we had assigned seating areas, the players could sit wherever they wanted, as the stadium was not sold out. We had a designated time and location for all of our players to report with two minutes left in the game.

Most of us were sitting in one end zone. A handful of the older players sat in the UCONN student section. We could see them and enjoyed watching them trying to interact with college students. One of our seniors, Tony Cortez, was a social butterfly. He was very polite and friendly. Tony reminded me of a good version of Eddie Haskell from the *Leave it to Beaver* television show.

The game went well for UCONN and they easily defeated Buffalo. As our team was gathering at the prearranged location, Tony showed up very excited. The other players who sat with Tony shared his enthusiasm.

Tony came running up to me with his usual broad smile on his face and enthusiastically said, "Coach Herman, why didn't you tell me college girls are so dang beautiful? Oh my God Coach! Had I known this before, I would have studied much harder so I could go to college."

We all had a good laugh. In fact, Tony did go to college after graduating. He played one semester of football at Bridgewater State College in Bridgewater, Massachusetts, but left after the first semester of his second year. He joined the Armed Forces, serving in the Army National Guard, for six years. Tony did not return to college.

I'd like to think the exposure we gave our athletes to college life, even for just one day, led to some of them being more excited and motivated about attending college. However, not all of our players went on to postsecondary education.

I found it interesting that a large number of our football athletes went into the U.S. Armed Forces, or joined law enforcement and other public service professions.

CHAPTER 17

"You guys line up alphabetically by height." - *Bill Peterson*

One aspect of the game is often overlooked. Special teams play can be the difference between winning or losing, especially when the two teams are evenly matched. We never just gave lip service to special teams. Because of our commitment to special teams, we won several games.

It was the first game of the 2009 football season. Dhonathan Lemos, a student from Brazil, was a senior and a three year football player. He had never seen or played American football until moving to Martha's Vineyard in his freshman year. He was now a starting defensive tackle. Dhonathan was short, thickly built, and sturdy. He was a polite, unassuming young man, with limited football knowledge, but he was an excellent right-footed, soccer style kicker.

In addition was Michael Araujo, a junior. Michael had played football for several years in youth league, junior high, and high school. Michael was a solid athlete and this year was one of our starting wide receivers, as well as our back up, right handed QB, a backup defensive back, and holder on field goals and extra points. Michael's uncle, David Araujo, a standout star in football and track when he was at MVRHS, was one of my varsity assistant coaches. In addition to David coaching defensive backs and receivers, another one of David's duties was coordinating special teams.

Coaching football allowed David the opportunity to spend quality time with his nephew.

During a typical week of practice we spent several ten minute periods working on specific special team plays. We'd spend ten minutes one day on punt and punt returns. One day we'd spend ten minutes on kickoffs and kickoff returns, as well as ten minutes on extra points and field goals. On a specific day of the week, usually a Wednesday before a Friday game, we would spend as much time as needed on special teams. In addition to these blocks of time, we did a ten minute specialist period twice a week. On the day before a game, we performed our usual pregame routine, which consisted of one of our ten minute specialty periods. Once we had completed our warm-up and other pregame activities, the team went through a mock game, situational practice. We tried to simulate game situations and scenarios during the weekly practices, especially on the day before a game. This one practice took roughly ninety minutes to complete. Included in these special team periods was the execution of field goals and extra points, from both ends of the field.

I'm trying to make the point that we dedicated ample time to special teams. Being sound in the special teams phase of the game can play a significant part in the outcome of the game. The week of practice leading up to our first game was nothing out of the ordinary.

We were playing Old Rochester at home on a beautiful Friday night. The first quarter went well for us. We scored a touchdown at the scoreboard end of the field. The extra point team ran onto the field.

We always aligned ourselves in the swinging gate alignment for extra points. What this meant for us, was we had our snapper, usually wearing an eligible receiver's number, the holder, and the kicker aligned over the ball in the middle of the field. On our left hash we had another receiver, split out, and aligned off the ball so that he and the snapper were both eligible receivers by number and alignment. On the right hash we had the rest of the extra point team. We aligned six men on the line of scrimmage, with the outside man being an eligible receiver. Behind them we had our two wing backs, both positioned behind the line, facing the holder.

We had set, designated plays, that could be executed for two points, depending on the adjustment the defense made to this formation. When we scored a touchdown, I signaled a number to the holder for the play I wanted to run. The holder then yelled that number out, and we executed the play on the snap of the ball.

After we scored that first touchdown, I signaled in the number one to Michael which meant when everyone was aligned in the swinging gate formation, Michael was to yell out, "One-one." The extra point team would run in and set up in the usual extra point formation. Once everyone was set, Michael signaled for the ball to be snapped. The center snapped the ball to the holder, and the kicker kicked the extra point. We did this and Dhonathan's kick was good, sailing right down the middle of the uprights with plenty of distance to spare. The first quarter ended with MV ahead 7-0.

It was now the second quarter, and we scored again, this time at the other end of the field, taking a 13-0 lead. Once again, the extra point team ran onto the field and immediately aligned itself in the swinging gate formation. Michael looked over at me and I gave the number one signal. Again, by calling number one, we had everyone run in, get set, snap the ball and kick the extra point.

However, as I was holding up the number one finger, I noticed something out of the ordinary from Michael. I saw him kneeling on the wrong side, the left side, of the black block kicking tee. Dhonathan set up on the same side, where he usually would be to kick the ball.

In my headset, I asked David, "What is your nephew doing on the left side of the block?" Not, what was my player doing on the left side?

David simply responded, "Coach, I haven't a clue."

I was forced to take a time out, something I never liked doing during a special teams play. Michael unassumingly jogged over to me on the sideline. Innocently, Michael asked, "Coach, what's up?"

I replied, "Michael, since when did Dhonathan become a left footed kicker?"

Michael looked dumbfounded and asked me what I meant. I told him, "You are kneeling on the wrong side of the block."

Michael responded with conviction by saying, "Coach, we scored a touchdown in the first quarter on the scoreboard end of the field, and I was on the right side of the block. We just scored a touchdown on the other side of the field, so I'm supposed to be on the other side of the block."

I looked at Michael as only a confused coach can, hands on my hip, shaking my head. I asked Michael, "What foot does Dhonathan kick the ball with? How is he going to do that with you being on the wrong side?" All of a sudden, the light went off in Michael's head.

Michael said, "Oh dang, my bad."

With that, I said to Michael, "You're an idiot." Michael smiled, turned and ran onto the field and we executed the kick, which once again, was good.

As Dhonathan ran over to the sideline to get the kickoff call, I asked him, "What was going through your mind when you saw Michael kneeling on the wrong side of the block?"

He just gave a large smile and said, "Coach, I was wondering what he was doing over there. I was about ready to switch sides and kick the ball with my left foot."

FYI, we won the game.

I often wondered if this sort of thing just happened to us or do other high school coaches suffer the same brain farts from their players? I'm willing to bet college and professional coaches don't have to wonder about these types of issues.

CHAPTER 18

"Mental toughness is going out there and doing what's best for the team—even though everything isn't going exactly the way you want it to." - Bill Belichick

When you coach a sport long enough, you find some seasons present more challenges than others. All teams must overcome adversity. The 2009 football season presented a series of obstacles. There were several unforeseen issues which made that season a memorable one, and not all the memories are fond ones.

The 2008 season was our last year in the Mayflower League. We were perennial league championship contenders. From 1991-2008, MV won eight Mayflower League titles, two co-championships and five Super Bowls in eight attempts. The 2008 team won the league championship but lost in the Super Bowl to Amesbury High School from Amesbury, Massachusetts. At the conclusion of that season, the *Boston Globe* named me Coach of the Year for our division, my first and only time receiving this honor.

During the winter of 2009, our school was invited to join the Eastern Athletic Conference (EAC). This league was comprised of three private Catholic high schools and one large public high school. Principal Steve Nixon sent out an email to all coaches at our school. This email allowed anyone not wanting to join this new league an opportunity to voice their concerns. I was the only coach to accept this invitation.

Participating in that meeting, was our athletic director, Mike Joyce,

Principal Steve Nixon and me. The athletic director was also the boys varsity basketball coach. I had just one question for our principal. "Why would football want or need to go into a league that has three private schools that recruit and one public school with over 1,000 students, while our enrollment was declining, going below 650 students?"

His response was, "They don't recruit, that's a violation."

I looked over at my AD and he said nothing. I laughed and asked, "Are you kidding me?" I then told them both, "We have worked too hard and sacrificed too much since 1988 to see this program fail. If we go into this league, it will destroy everything we've done here and eventually destroy the football program." Those concerns fell on deaf ears. The 2009 season would be our first in the EAC.

In 2008 there were seventy-five players on our team. Our first year in the EAC, we were down to fifty-nine. Our numbers would decline every year until my last year in 2015 where we finished with just thirty-eight players.

Adversity struck again in late July.

I always took on the responsibility of making the football schedule. Once I received my league schedule, I began filling in the open dates. For MV this meant building from the back forward. The last regular season game with Nantucket was always a given.

Hosting the Island Cup is a significant undertaking. The Island Cup game traditionally draws the largest crowd to attend any sporting event for both schools.

This game is so popular that several major national magazines have written about it: *Yankee Magazine*, *Life Magazine*, *The New York Times*, and *US Sports*. The rivalry is talked about on sports talk radio, covered by Boston and local newspapers, and has even been featured on half-time shows on national TV during both college and professional football games. I received emails every summer from people as far away as California wanting to know the exact date and location of the next Island Cup game. They were already making plans to attend the game. This game is a big deal.

It was late July in 2009 when I received an email from the Nantucket

Boys and Girls Club director. His email asked, "When and where are we playing the junior high football game this year seeing as our two high school teams aren't playing?"

My immediate email reply was, "What the hell are you talking about? They're on my schedule."

I forwarded that email to my AD, to my principal, and to the Nantucket AD. Nantucket did not respond.

On August eighth while working my summer job on South Beach for the town of Edgartown I ran into a former junior varsity football coach from Nantucket and asked him, "What the hell are you doing over here?"

He replied, "Hey, the rumor has it we aren't playing each other in football this year."

I told him, "You're the second person in two weeks who said that. What the hell is going on?"

He just said, "This is what people on Nantucket are saying."

It's important to know that I was also an assistant softball coach at MVRHS. The Nantucket AD was their head softball coach. We had seen each other on three different occasions that previous spring. We played each other twice and we both attended the same preseason softball jamboree. Their AD/softball coach never said a word about us not playing football.

On August eighth I called the Nantucket AD and asked, "What is the deal? When was anyone going to let me know, November sixteenth?" The game was to be played on MV on November twenty-third.

We had a spirited conversation for roughly twenty-five minutes. The Nantucket AD stated that other Nantucket coaches had been complaining that they weren't playing the Vineyard.

He said, "There are concerns about a Title IV violation and seeing that our two schools no longer used planes to get to each other, the cost of the fan boat was going to be too expensive."

After hearing their AD use the cost of the boat as a reason for not playing, I responded, "The boat is not an excuse. You will be able to pay for the boat. In fact, I bet it will take less than one hour and someone will sponsor the boat."

He then went back to talking about how other fall sport teams wanted to play the Vineyard. He told me, "If we can play each other this year in soccer and field hockey, then we can play football too."

I almost dropped the phone. The AD had just finished saying that they could not afford the boat for one game. Now, if we played them in two more sports, all of a sudden the money was there to play football? I asked the AD for the real reason they didn't want to play us this year but I never received a valid response.

Early in 2009 the only football coach Nantucket ever had, the legendary and Hall of Famer Vito Capizzo, retired. The new coach was former star player, John Aloisi. John was a three year starter at QB for Nantucket from 1993-1995, beating the Vineyard in each of those years.

After hanging up with the Nantucket AD, I was agitated. The 2009 Island Cup was supposed to be a home game for us. It most likely would have been a win as well. My youngest child, Gail, was a senior that year. She would have had bragging rights that she was the only Herman child to see the Vineyard beat Nantucket on the Vineyard. My two other children saw the Vineyard beat Nantucket in their senior years. However, both of those games were played on Nantucket.

Practice was set to start in just a couple of weeks. Most, if not all, high schools in Massachusetts have their ten or eleven game schedule set and filled by then. The question then became, "Who was I going to schedule in place of Nantucket?"

I immediately started making phone calls to anyone who appeared to have the last week of the season open. Of the schools I contacted none of them wanted to travel to the Vineyard and play us. The travel money was not in their budget. We even offered to pay their boat expense.

I began looking into nearby states for schools that were available. I came across one in Providence, RI. Their AD agreed to play us. What a relief. Now with at least a game to complete our schedule, I had to face the task of telling my seniors that there was not going to be an Island Cup game.

I conducted a meeting each year three days before the start of practice with just the seniors. It was at this meeting that I gave them the bad news. Keep in mind that I had seen most of those seniors grow up since elementary school. I was close to many of them.

When boys play football on Martha's Vineyard (and I am sure it is the same on Nantucket), they start looking forward to playing in the Island Cup game, especially when it is at home in their senior year. Through no fault of their own, seniors from both islands were going to be denied that rite of passage.

During the meeting with my seniors, I went over the usual information that I cover every year. Once I had finished, I began breaking the bad news to them. I explained the events that had occurred, and I told them there would not be an Island Cup game this year. Some players began to swear, but most players started crying. I don't know for sure, but I expect the scene was the same on Nantucket.

The season began and was going according to the plan. We lost our first game to a better team but then ran off several consecutive wins.

On a Tuesday morning in the middle of October, I received a phone call from the AD at the Rhode Island school that was replacing Nantucket. He told me that his school would no longer be able to play us. I was dumbfounded. Here it was mid-October, and once again I had to try and fill our schedule for the last week of the season. I immediately started making phone calls to any school that appeared to have that weekend open.

Fortunately, I came across Brighton High School in Boston. They had just a nine game schedule and did not have a game scheduled for the weekend I needed. I knew their head football coach, Timo Philip. We first met coaching together in the Shriners North-South All-Star football game two years prior. Brighton came to the Vineyard in 2008 for a preseason scrimmage.

I immediately contacted the Boston school's athletic director. I explained our situation and asked if he would permit Brighton to play us that November weekend. I had already talked with Timo and he was on board. The Boston AD approved the game, both junior varsity and varsity. Thank God! Timo and I made arrangements for his team to come over the Friday night before the game. MV Touchdown Club agreed to feed both teams. Their players were scheduled to stay with families of my players. On the morning of the games, MV Touchdown Club provided breakfast for both teams. It would be a great cultural exchange and opportunity for both schools.

With a game now confirmed for the last week, I could turn my full attention toward our next opponent, Seekonk High School. We had not played Seekonk since the 1997 season when we beat them soundly. We were playing at Seekonk that weekend.

Seekonk High School is well over an hour away by school bus and don't forget the forty-five minute boat ride before the bus ride. Halfway there I started hearing that one of my starting linemen, sophomore Max Moreis, was not feeling well. I passed it off as him having motion sickness.

We arrived at the school and were provided a small locker room. Our team of roughly fifty-nine players was crammed into a tiny space. We had to dress in shifts. Once we were all dressed, we left for the game field together.

Our pregame went off without a hitch. However, once again I was told that Max was not feeling well. I went to Max and asked how he was doing. He told me, "I'm fine, just having some stomach issues." We both thought it was pregame nerves. He continued, "I'll be okay once the game starts."

The game went well for us. We ended up winning by a close score against a staunch opponent. After the game I once again asked Max how he was feeling. He said, "I think I have a fever and am coming down with something."

I don't know how many of you have been on a school bus. It is cramped and you sit almost on top of each other. That day, our school bus became an incubator of sorts.

The next day, Saturday, I called to see how Max was doing. He had gone to the hospital that night with a high fever. They diagnosed Max with the swine flu.

On Sunday afternoon my coaches met to go over the game film and prepare for our next opponent, Cape Tech. Cape Tech was a program that was struggling.

As I left the coaches meeting, I received a phone call from another player's parent. Their son was experiencing the same symptoms as Max. I told them to go to the hospital. Sure enough, the player was diagnosed with the swine flu. Roughly two hours later, a third player called to say that, he too, had the swine flu. Now we had three confirmed cases of the flu in two days. Before Tuesday over twenty-five percent of my team was out with the swine flu. In addition to the MV football team, several other fall sport teams were suffering from the same illness.

With so many students and athletes out with this flu, the school administration considered canceling all sports that week. We were allowed to hold practice that Monday and Tuesday.

PURPLE PRIDE

On Wednesday afternoon, just after lunch period, I was called into the AD's office. I walked into the office and saw the school nurse, the AD, the athletic trainer, and the principal. I recall thinking it was odd that the principal was there. I asked, "Did I not get the invitation? Who's the party for?"

They invited me to that party to inform me that due to the high rate of illness, the weekend football game at Cape Tech would be canceled. The AD was concerned about how I would respond to the news. She had asked for reinforcements.

What she didn't know was that I had anticipated our game being canceled. It is important to note that Martha's Vineyard was not the only community exposed to the swine flu. It had become a nationwide epidemic.

Not only were we not going to have a game that weekend, we weren't even allowed to conduct practice. Our school has a policy that states that if twenty-five percent of the team is out of school, the remaining team cannot hold practice or have games. We would have to wait until our percentage dropped below that twenty-five percent.

We were not able to conduct a practice until the Wednesday of the following week. We were scheduled to play a league game at Bishop Stang that Friday. They had not suffered any flu issues and were able to play the weekend before our game. The game with Bishop Stang was going to be our third league game. We were 1-1 in our new league, the Eastern Athletic Conference (EAC).

Somehow, after taking a week off from football, our kids rallied and we beat a solid Bishop Stang squad. We were set to play Somerset in our last league game the next weekend. If we won, we would claim a share of the league championship. We ended up losing by a significant margin to an outstanding Somerset squad.

In looking back on that year, many things come to mind. Our team left the comfort of the Mayflower League and entered the unknown of the EAC. We finished that first season 2-2 in the EAC. We would never exceed that league win-loss ratio, sometimes going 1-3. Nor would we qualify for another postseason run.

Our team and school came down with the swine flu. Who would have ever thought something like that would happen? After all, isn't the flu considered a wintertime illness? We missed one game but bounced back and won a game after having just two practices.

Of course it was a nightmare and a disappointment not having an Island Cup game. I vividly remember walking out to the game field that day. Even though the weather was beautiful and Brighton had agreed in the eleventh hour to make the trip to the Vineyard, something just did not feel right. The junior varsity was playing. The grounds and stands were decorated purple and white and the stadium was full of spectators. We held our senior recognition before kickoff. We played the games and both Vineyard teams won. Finally, the season was over.

During that year the 2009 team stayed focused and remained driven, mainly due to the leadership of those seniors. We finished this season from hell with a very respectable 7–3 record.

"Adversity has the effect of eliciting talents which in prosperous circumstances would have lain dormant." — Horace. I first heard this quote when Todd Araujo, a senior leader on the 1989 team, used it in the football highlight video after that team lost its only game of the year.

I always told my players that the ability to overcome adversity, whatever the form, is critical to being successful. We are all faced with challenges on a daily basis. You either succumb or you overcome.

I am proud of that 2009 football team. That team faced every adversity head on and won.

In my Panthers uniform, 10 years old.

Brother Lettermen, December, 1974.

At our wedding shower, 1984.

My last meal as a single man.
L-R: Bobby, Mama, Daddy, Barbara.

Proud parents, Samuel and Archee Herman, June 23, 1984.

Herman Crosses the Sound.

The cartoon that appeared in the papers the day before my first Island Cup game on Nantucket, 1988. Artwork by Gus D'Angelo, Vineyard Gazette.

Celebrating my first Island Cup win in 1989. Pictured with Louis Paciello. Photo by Mark Alan Lovewell, Vineyard Gazette.

During a timeout in the 1991 Super Bowl with Jason Tilman, Rusty Ventura and Cameron Cuch. Photo by Mark Alan Lovewell, Vineyard Gazette.

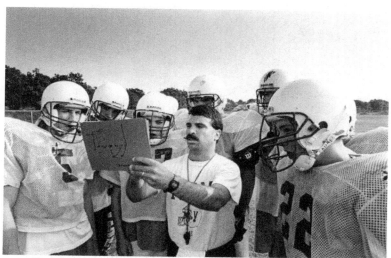

Defensive scout session during a practice in 1992. Photo by Mark Alan Lovewell, Vineyard Gazette.

Island Cup coin toss on Nantucket, 1992. One of the Vineyards most exciting victories in the Island Cup series. L-R: Jason Dyer, Sam Hayes, Rusty Ventura, Albie Robinson.

My family enjoying a fall day in Chilmark, 1998.
L-R: Gail, Adam, Eric, Pam.

EJ Sylvia kicks game winner, 2004 Island Cup.
Photo by Cape Cod Times.

The ultimate 12th Man and water boy, 2004. Photo by Nicole Harnishfeger, The Inquirer and Mirror.

Coach B holds the Cup after beating Nantucket, 2005. L-R: Tristan Atwood, John Swann, Coach Bill Belcher, Anthony Sullo, Tony Cortez. Photo by Ralph Stewart, MV Times.

Adam, Gail and Eric during the summer of 2010 on Circuit Ave, Oak Bluffs. Pam and I became empty nesters when Gail started at UCONN.

Cooler dump after shutting out Nantucket. Coaches and former
players, Jason O'Donnell and Neil Estrella try to stay dry.
Photo by David Welch, MV Times.

The victors being welcomed back, 2013.
Photo by David Welch, MV Times.

Jacob Cardoza makes the game winning catch, 2014 Island Cup. Photo by Michael Cummo, MV Times.

Hall of Fame Induction Ceremony, April, 2015. Eric, Yasmín, Pam, Gail, and Adam. Photo by Dave Araujo, DJR Photos.

Cooler dump after shutting out Nantucket. Coaches and former
players, Jason O'Donnell and Neil Estrella try to stay dry.
Photo by David Welch, MV Times.

The victors being welcomed back, 2013.
Photo by David Welch, MV Times.

Jacob Cardoza makes the game winning catch, 2014 Island Cup. Photo by Michael Cummo, MV Times.

Hall of Fame Induction Ceremony, April, 2015. Eric, Yasmín, Pam, Gail, and Adam. Photo by Dave Araujo, DJR Photos.

Honored at half-time from former players along with banners they were part of winning. Photo by Sam Moore, MV Times.

Fans wore fake purple mustaches at my last game on Nantucket. L-R: Gail, Pam, Yasmín, Eric. Adam not pictured.

Jacob and I enjoy celebrating our last game, a win over Nantucket, 2015. Photo by Paul Cardoza.

A heroes welcome. Photo by Sam Moore, MV Times.

Legendary, retired and Hall of Fame coach from Nantucket, Vito Capizzo and I enjoying an Island Cup game, on MV, from the sidelines. November, 2016. Sadly, this would be the last time I would see Vito alive before his passing in May of 2018. Photo by Sam Moore, MV Times.

Our first grandchild, Jason Emil Herman. Eric and Yasmín
are the proud parents.

T-shirt designed by Peter Lambos, Class of 1998.
Amazing the resemblance.

CHAPTER 19

"Two things are infinite: the universe and human stupidity, and I'm not sure about the universe." - Albert Einstein

Starting in the summer of 1996, I helped run an instructional football camp on the island for grades 7-12. One of my assistant coaches, Mike McCarthy, came up with the idea. In other local areas football players could easily attend football camps, participate in 7-on-7 competitions, but not the kids from Martha's Vineyard.

Most kids on the Vineyard start working summer jobs at the age of fourteen. In order to attend any off-island camp or training session, a player must leave work early. They then take the forty-five minute ferry ride to Woods Hole, and find round trip transportation to that camp. Traveling back and forth from the Vineyard, especially in the summer, was not practical.

Our instructional camp always began the last week in July. It ran from 5:30 p.m. to 7:30 p.m., Monday through Friday. As this was a noncontact camp, we only issued shoulder pads and helmets to our participants. The camp registration and insurance coverage was managed through the high school summer school program.

It was the July 2010 session and we had just completed a successful camp week. One of my parting comments to my returning players was that we started official football practice in two weeks. Those comments included a reminder to be sure to stay out of trouble.

It's essential to the story to know that I also had a full-time, 9 a.m. to 5 p.m., summer job. Since the summer of 1989 I've worked for the Edgartown Parks Department on South Beach. For the first five years of my residency on the Vineyard, I was the beach director and was in charge of roughly twenty lifeguards. We were responsible for a mile long stretch of beach between the right and left forks on the south facing shoreline of Martha's Vineyard. South Beach is known for its shore breaks, rip currents, and rough surf. There are also days when the water was so calm the beach had the nickname of Lake Katama. Katama is the section of Edgartown near South Beach.

In my first year as the beach director, my lifeguards made sixty-three saves, including twelve in one day. That year was the extreme for there are some summers that the lifeguards never have to enter the water to assist or save swimmers.

After those five summers I decided to pass the torch to a younger person. However, I stayed on with the Edgartown Parks Department and became a full-time member of the beach patrol for the same stretch of beach. My job entailed making sure the beach was clean and maintained each day, supporting the guards with crowd control and rescues, keeping the beachgoers safe, and being a good PR person for the island and the town of Edgartown. One of the perks of both of my jobs on South Beach was being able to ride up and down the beach on a four-wheel drive ATV. Another perk was getting paid to get a tan.

As I previously stated, our instructional camp ended and my last message to my players was to stay out of trouble.

On the first Sunday after our camp, around 3:00 p.m., I was riding my ATV on the beach. It was not unusual to see several of my former players and students at South Beach. Especially on Sundays, it was not uncommon for beachgoers to have grills and cookouts on the beach.

One such grill was in operation near the right fork. The grill chef, a former student of mine, invited me over for a hotdog. Being one who never turns down free food, I parked my ATV to the side of the grill so that I was still facing the water, able to see the swimmers and other beachgoers. As I was sitting on my ATV, I looked about ten yards to my right and saw some current and former athletes enjoying the beautiful summer day. Sitting in a lounge chair with his back to me was none other than Michael. Michael, who was going to be a senior on that year's team, a four-year team member, was enjoying the afternoon on South Beach. I looked over in time to see what I thought was a motion to drink from a can and see a puff of smoke coming from the lounge chair.

I initially thought nothing of this, saying to myself, "No way." Keep in mind two of Michael's friends were standing next to him in a position so that they could easily see me. I continued having my hotdog and carrying on a conversation with my host. Once again I looked over in Michael's direction. I saw him take a drink, put the can on the ground, and saw another puff of smoke.

This time I got off of my ATV. I walked over to where Michael was sitting and saw him again reach beside him, lift a can of Budweiser, take a sip, and put the beer can back on the ground. He then raised a Swisher Sweet cigar to his lips and took a puff. All of this happened within two feet of me. Either Michael didn't know I was there or he didn't care. I didn't bother asking.

As I was approaching him, his friends began moving away because I think they knew what was coming. I walked right up to Michael and started yelling at him, "What the hell do you think you are doing? I can't believe what I am seeing. You can't be that stupid but that's a rhetorical question, and I know you don't know what that means. Get your butt off of this beach right now." I think people within a quarter of a mile were able to hear me yelling.

To Michael's credit, he didn't say anything. He quickly got up, left his beer, cigar, and chair, and walked off the beach with his head down. Roughly ten minutes later, after I calmed down a little, I contacted David, Michael's uncle and one of my assistant coaches. I started telling David what had just happened.

David replied, "I already heard."

At the senior players meeting two weeks later, I covered the expectations and goals for the upcoming season. I then turned my attention to Michael. Most of the seniors had heard about the incident on the beach and were anxiously awaiting what I was going to do. At our grass practice field, in one end zone, we had five tires that were half-buried. Those tires represented the five offensive linemen. We used those tires to work on defensive alignment and drills. Because of the way the tires were installed, lawnmowers can't get close enough to mow the grass between or around them. Each year the tires were covered with grass.

I explained that if the beach incident had occurred once official practice had started, Michael would have been thrown off the team. Since this incident happened before we had started, Michael would be allowed to play. However, before he could begin practice, I had a job for him to complete.

In my back pocket I had a pair of scissors. I pulled the scissors out and handed them to Michael. He looked at them in wonderment. I told Michael, "The grass at the tires needs cutting. You have until the start of practice Thursday to get this done to my liking." All of Michael's classmates started roaring with laughter. Michel looked at me as if I must be joking.

Although I did not make Michael perform that duty, I did make him responsible for carrying the heavy headset container to all away games.

I used this incident as a teaching moment for the rest of the team. That was the last time I caught a player drinking or smoking in front of me.

CHAPTER 20

"I've found prayers work best when you have big players." - Knute Rockne

Each year our team participated in two or three preseason scrimmages. In 2008 we faced nineteen different high schools, including the various teams we scrimmaged and played against. One of those schools was the Harlem Hellfighters from Harlem, New York. They came to Martha's Vineyard for a game scrimmage on Labor Day weekend.

David Currid, head coach at Cape Tech in Harwich, Massachusetts contacted me with the idea of scrimmaging Harlem. He was attending a coaches clinic in Texas when he met the Harlem head coach, Duke Fergerson. Coach Fergerson was looking for a scrimmage opponent from the Cape and David immediately thought about Martha's Vineyard.

Coach Fergerson, who had played in the NFL for the Dallas Cowboys and Seattle Seahawks, and I talked over the phone and worked out the details. They arrived on the Friday afternoon of Labor Day weekend. Few, if any, of the Harlem players had ever seen the ocean before, much less ever been on a boat, so the forty-five minute boat ride from Woods Hole to Martha's Vineyard was a brand new experience.

I met the team in Oak Bluffs. Transportation had been arranged, as was always the case for a visiting team. The school buses brought the Harlem team to the high school. Once there, I was asked if I had any extra equipment for a couple of their team members. I walked the players over to our equipment room and started handing out a few pieces of equipment. Before I knew it, I looked up and nearly their entire team was there needing gear. I gladly passed out what was needed.

We had plans to practice together that Friday afternoon. After the practice I assigned their players housing with my players. One player, Q, had to stay with an assistant coach. Q was not a problem kid. He just didn't understand personal space. Q was a 6'6", 280 pound junior lineman. The coaches were concerned that if Q went into town with his host player, he would stand too close to someone, invading their personal space, and the potential for an altercation would occur.

Q and a couple of the Harlem coaches came to my house after practice to shower and go out for dinner at a local restaurant.

There are two indoor and one outdoor showers at my house. I showed Q the outdoor shower. When I first told Q he was taking his shower outside, he looked at me as if I was crazy. I think he thought I was just going to hand him a hose and a bar of soap. However, once I showed him the enclosed shower, he was satisfied.

After I came inside and took my shower, as did one of the assistant coaches, I started asking if Q had come back inside. He had not. I went in the backyard to check. I yelled out, "Q, are you okay?"

He responded, "Coach, this is great. This is awesome." As Q was coming out of the shower, he looked up and asked me, "What are those?"

I looked up and all I saw were stars. I told Q those are stars. He said he'd never seen them before. Sadly, this was his life in the city.

The next day we had a successful scrimmage with Harlem. Both teams enjoyed the experience. My touchdown club provided a cookout for both teams and we had a group picture taken together. Harlem left the island on an afternoon boat after having a wonderful experience on Martha's Vineyard.

That cultural exchange remains one of my fondest memories. The young men from Harlem conducted themselves with class and as gentlemen. Some of our parents asked if we could host them again the following year. Unfortunately, the Harlem program was unable to sustain itself and the team was disbanded shortly after that 2008 season.

Starting in 1996 one scrimmage that we annually participated in was at Mashpee High School in Mashpee, Massachusetts. Mashpee, Martha's Vineyard, and Sandwich High School were the annual participants. From time to time, a fourth high school would join. Other high schools that joined in over the years were Austin Prep, Dennis-Yarmouth, and Upper Cape.

In 2014 Nantucket asked if they could participate. Nantucket's original scrimmage opponent had to cancel. We had beaten Nantucket eleven years in a row, and they had just hired a new head coach. I told Matt Triveri, the Mashpee head coach and athletic director, "I don't object to Nantucket coming, but we won't scrimmage them."

On this day MV and Mashpee were the first schools to warm up and start. Sandwich usually arrived later, as they were already in school. Nantucket also came late due to their boat schedule. While Sandwich was warming up and Nantucket still not there, MV and Mashpee were conducting a noncontact passing session.

Sandwich arrived before Nantucket and once they were ready, we started the controlled scrimmage. In a controlled scrimmage coaches are allowed on the field and in the huddle. A full crew of referees are there working the scrimmage. A controlled scrimmage is for learning purposes. Coaches can stop the play at any time and review plays with their team.

Nantucket finally arrived. Martha's Vineyard started the scrimmage with Mashpee as Nantucket was commencing their warm-ups. Sandwich was on the sidelines awaiting their turn.

One of the calisthenics Nantucket did was jumping jacks. While doing their jumping jacks, they were yelling out the number of reps by counting from one to fifteen for each jumping jack. We were on the sideline while this was happening, as Mashpee and Sandwich were now scrimmaging each other.

As the Nantucket players were counting and yelling the numbers out loud, one of my new players asked, "What are they yelling out?"

Ben Clark, a junior and three-year starter quickly responded, "They are counting the number of years we've beaten them in a row."

We all had a good laugh and enjoyed a successful scrimmage.

CHAPTER 21

"Common sense is like deodorant, those who need it the most never use it." –
Anonymous

In July of the mid 2010's, a player from our junior high football team participated in our instructional football camp. He had a successful eighth grade season while playing quarterback on our junior high football team. The same player was at our instructional camp as an incoming freshman. He was a solid athlete and showed potential at playing QB for the high school.

Our regular season began three weeks after our camp ended. We issued equipment three days before our first day of official practice. During those three days I did not see that young freshman come back to pick up the rest of his equipment. I started hearing rumors and was worried that he was not going to play.

On the morning of the day before our season started, I called that player's father. The father told me that their family decided that his son was not going to play football. I said, "But he did the camp."

The father responded with, "Yes. He did the camp knowing he wasn't going to play."

I had a hard time comprehending that line of thinking and asked, "What is your real issue?" He was concerned that his son was too small and vulnerable to injury. Before I hung up, I was able to convince both of this player's parents to meet with my junior varsity coach and me later that day.

PURPLE PRIDE

Jason Neago, my head junior varsity coach, had played football and graduated from the United States Air Force Academy. Jason was in his second year as a science teacher at the high school. He was an assistant junior varsity coach in his first year, and this was going to be Jason's second year involved in our program.

Jason and I met with the parents at the high school game field. Their concerns, mostly the moms, were over her son's safety. After several minutes of talking back and forth, the mom finally said, "Okay, you are starting to win me over. How about we do this? Do whatever you want with my son during practice. Run him all you want, but can you not play him in the games?"

Of course that request caught me off guard. I looked over at Jason who also looked confused. My immediate response was, "Two things: number one that's not happening and number two, have you run this idea by your son?"

I could not see how a young, talented, competitive player would be okay with working hard all week in practice but not play in games. The mom took about five seconds after hearing my two points and finally said her son could play. Her son came later that day and picked up the rest of his equipment.

He played his freshman year. Even though he wasn't the starter, he did see plenty of game action at QB. He played just that one year.

I firmly believe that some parents are overprotective. In my opinion, if a child wishes to participate in a healthy activity, parents should be supportive. I don't know for sure, but I am willing to bet that specific mother was putting thoughts in her son's head during the season about not getting hurt. I've always been of the opinion that if you think about getting hurt, you will get hurt.

Parents need to know that the window of being involved in their child's life is always closing. Parents should be encouraging and become involved with their child's activities. Children want their parents there supporting them, even if they say they don't.

Having been involved with high school football and other sports for thirty-five years, and being a father of three, I learned that parents who actively engage with their children have kids that, more often than not, excel in all realms of education. Those kid's grades are higher, they rarely get into trouble, and they are more likely to continue their education after high school.

I told parents all the time, "Please come and be active in your child's high school career. Once those years are over, they're over. You don't get that time back."

CHAPTER 22

"Sometimes I wish I was an octopus, so I could slap eight people at once." -Anonymous

One Saturday morning in late September, in my first year of retirement, my wife and I had just finished having breakfast together. Pam was in her last year of teaching fourth grade before she would be retiring. She wasn't excited to still be teaching while I was at home. Apparently when she got home, she needed her space.

As I was washing the breakfast dishes, Pam turned to me and said, "You know all those years you spent away from the family coaching football? I really hated that you were gone so much. Now you are home all the time. I really hate that you are always home."

I responded with, "Damn, I can't win." We both laughed. However, she did say, "You really need to get a hobby or find something to do."

Admittedly, I was starting to get a little bored. The honey-do list was starting to shrink. My days consisted of going to the beach, working around the house taking care of things that had been neglected for years, and going to the local YMCA to exercise. I also took care of our dog, Mowgli.

In my opinion, September is one of the best times to be on Martha's Vineyard. The weather is great. Shops are still open. Traffic is much lighter, so finding a place to park is easier and the beaches are still nice.

Nevertheless, after a couple of cloudy days in a row, I decided to ask

Asil Cash, Director of Health and Wellness at the YMCA, if there were any openings for a trainer. Asil was a former player of mine.

Asil was excited about having me join the staff. With my background of thirty-five years teaching physical education and coaching, he thought I could be a positive addition to the YMCA family.

I began working at the Y covering the floor a couple of days a week. I also took over the two group exercise classes that my son and daughter-in-law, Eric and Yasmín, had started two years prior. They had recently moved to Charlotte, North Carolina.

In addition to covering the floor and running exercise classes, I took on clients to train and I participated in other group exercise classes, as well as doing my own workouts.

In December of 2017, I was training a graduating senior from the MVRHS football team, Cooper Bennett. I donated training sessions to the MV Touchdown Club's annual auction. Cooper's parents purchased this donation.

During one of our early workout times, Cooper was exhausted and had yet to finish the training session. I reminded Cooper (who played for me my last two years as the head coach) that I was big on conditioning and discipline. He said, "Oh, I know," and proceeded to remind me of the following story, which I had forgotten. Actually, Cooper not only jarred my memory of this story but of another one that occurred near the end of the season.

In 2015, my last season, we were having a morning session during the first week of practice. We had a veteran team. Several of my seniors had two years of playing experience. One of these seniors was Ben Clark, a two-way starter at fullback and inside linebacker. Ben had also seen some varsity playing time at linebacker when he was a freshman.

That morning was a defensive practice. We were doing a perimeter period. That was a drill with our defensive perimeter players (defensive backs and linebackers) running our pass coverages against an opponent's offensive perimeter (receivers and running backs). I was insistent that our defensive players communicate with each other when they saw that the play was a pass. I wanted my players, especially my linebackers, to yell out "pass" several times on pass plays.

It is vital to this story to know that Ben Clark was talkative, some would

even say, obnoxious. I often told Ben that he spewed verbal vomit. The coaches referred to Ben as the head of the law firm of Clark and Clark.

During that perimeter period, which was mostly a pass oriented session, Ben was not yelling out, "pass," and neither was anyone else. Consequently, I was getting annoyed and gave them all a final warning. I made all of the defensive players perform ten pushups on the last play, when nobody communicated. After another play, with Ben not calling out, "Pass," I immediately stopped the session and had the entire group, offense, and defense, run two gassers.

Gassers are performed by dividing the group into two units, each on their own sideline. I'd blow my whistle, and both groups would run from one sideline to the other, bend down, touch the sideline paint, and sprint back. Down and back, down and back counted as one gasser.

I told them that we were running gassers, because Ben Clark forgot how to talk.

Apparently having the team run gassers for Ben's lack of communication made a lasting impression on at least one young player. We did, however, start doing a much better job of communicating after that point.

The other event took place in week ten of our eleven week schedule. We were playing at Norwell High School and arrived early after traveling for nearly two hours on the school bus. Almost everyone on the bus was in need of the bathroom.

As the bus drove up to the Norwell gymnasium, their AD greeted us. I explained our immediate need and he told us we could use his team's locker room facilities, since our team's changing area did not have bathroom facilities. His team members had not arrived at the school yet.

As our players and coaching staff poured into the locker room, we passed a large, white dry erase board that appeared to have our entire offensive and defensive playbooks drawn on it. In addition to our schemes being on the board, they had a handful of our players jersey numbers written on the board with comments about each one. A couple of examples were, "#28 – very strong runner, #22 – can score from anywhere."

There were also funny ones that had our team and coaches laughing.

Two of my senior linemen, Jimmy and Andy DiMattia, were identical twins. They were built the same, walked the same, and played the same.

They were listed on the board as, "#53, #56 – very good linemen, very similar."

On the board there was also a note about James. He was a junior tight end/defensive end. James was 6'6" and weighed 245 pounds and wore jersey #18. All season long I had been telling James that he needed to play to his size and athletic ability. I guess Norwell saw some of the same things in James that I saw. On the board they listed, "#18 – soft."

For the rest of the day, the team continually reminded James what Norwell thought of him. Maybe having someone outside our program bring this opinion to James' attention woke him up. All I know is that there was nothing soft about the way James played against Norwell or the following week in the Island Cup game. We won both games.

CHAPTER 23

"You have to expect things from yourself before you can do them." -
Michael Jordan

Unquestionably there are many events during the course of one's career that leave indelible impressions. One of these occurred in the 2015 season, my last year.

It was a Wednesday, the fifth week of the season, and we were 2-2, 1-1 in the Eastern Athletic Conference. We were coming off a tough 3-0 loss to perennial power Bishop Feehan.

On this day I was performing my teaching duty, one period every other day, as lunchroom monitor. After the third lunch period one of the assistant principals, Elliott Bennett, approached me. She told me that one of my star senior players, a captain, had recently cut a class. Another senior starter had also cut class. Both of them had cut classes on other days.

She explained to me that the players were going to serve an after school detention sometime in the near future. I did not get a chance during their lunch period to ask these players about this accusation, but planned to meet with them before practice that afternoon.

At the end of the last class period, I heard these two senior players names on the intercom asking them to report to the front office. When I heard these names, I got a feeling in my gut that something wasn't right.

On Wednesdays we didn't start practice until 3:30 p.m. We got out of school at 2:05. At 3:30 the varsity players returned for a film session before the start of our 5:00 practice under the lights.

At 2:05 I walked to the front office to find out why two of my senior players had been called to the office. The office personnel told me that the two of them had not only cut their last period class that day but had left the school grounds. I immediately knew I had to take strong and swift action.

As it approached 3:30, I was waiting near the classroom where the team was to report. One of the accused players, my captain, walked into the building as if nothing was wrong. I instructed him to come to my office. Once there I asked the young man, "So, how was last period today?"

He told me the truth, which was, "I went to a different class and then left school. I went home to get clothes for practice."

Seeing as this was now his third time cutting a class and that he was a captain and a leader on the team, I decided not to allow him to play in that week's game. In fact, as this was an away game, I was not going to let him travel with the team. In addition he had already earned his purple stripe for his helmet, a weekly award given out for various reasons. I told him to remove his purple pride stripe. I then said that I did not want to see him at practice until the first one the following week. He was to bring his equipment bag every day to that week's practices for some extra attitude adjustment conditioning. After the first player left my office, the second one arrived. I repeated the same conversation and enforced the same discipline.

When I got home after practice that night, I called and spoke with a parent of both players. While speaking with the captain's mother, I told her about the punishment, how disappointed I was, and that I had also decided to strip her son of his captainship. The problem was I never told the player this in person. That was a mistake on my part. Obviously, the mother was upset. She thought I was overreacting by taking her sons' captainship away. If the player was upset, he never mentioned it to me. He took his punishment in stride.

We played the game that week against another EAC team, Bishop Stang and lost 14-0. That game was played in a torrential downpour which also included a one and a half hour lightning delay which caused us to miss the last boat back to Martha's Vineyard. That alone would make for another story. We did, however, make it back to the Vineyard just after midnight. Needless to say, this game and week did not go according to my plan.

Could we have won the game with those two seniors playing? It is possible; however, school and academics come first. I have high standards that I expected my athletes to strive to achieve. I expected all of my players to be of strong character and always do what was right. I wanted my players to be solid citizens and positive examples in their communities. I would never sacrifice my beliefs for a win.

By the following week we were 2-3 and eliminated from league championship and playoff contention. We still had six games remaining. The two boys came to each practice and did their required runs and were reinstated into the starting lineup for the next game, Homecoming.

The player who had his captainship removed was four year starter, Jacob Cardoza. After thinking about Jacob's situation further, I decided to give him a chance to regain his captainship. One week earlier I had passed out progress report sheets for all players to take around and have their teachers complete. I saw Jacob's grades and was pleasantly surprised at how well he was doing academically.

Knowing that Jacob desperately wanted to become captain again, I made a deal with him. It is important to know that Jacob struggled with his grades and had never earned honor roll distinction at any time in school. So I offered to Jacob that if he made the first quarter honor roll, I would reinstate him as a captain. Jacob enthusiastically accepted the challenge.

Three weeks later our team's record was 4-4 with three remaining games. Our upcoming game was our last home game of the year and the one when we conducted our senior recognition ceremony.

The first academic quarter came to a close the afternoon of that game. I told Jacob that once the quarter ended, I would have all of his teachers report his grades to me. All of his grades were strong, but two classes were going to be close. Before the end of school that day, all of his teachers turned Jacob's grades in to me.

On that game day the players were scheduled to return to school at 3:00. Jacob came into the classroom where the team was to report. I addressed the team and explained the arrangement that I made with Jacob.

I was proud to announce that Jacob made the first quarter honor roll and was once again a captain. I told Jacob to wait to inform his parents until they were in line together for senior recognition.

Everyone in that room was excited for Jacob. He had accomplished two difficult goals: making honor roll and being renamed a team captain. We were all proud of Jacob and the message he was able to send to the entire team.

We were now 6-4 and heading into our last game of the year against Nantucket. That would be Jacob's final high school football game, as well as the last game of my coaching career.

We won the game 7-0. That win was the Vineyard's thirteenth consecutive year beating Nantucket and keeping the Island Cup.

Jacob had a thirty yard touchdown run called back on a questionable holding penalty, but played inspired football on both sides of the ball. In fact, the entire team played with motivation. They did not want to be known as the first Vineyard team to lose to Nantucket since 2002 and they did not want me to end my coaching career with a loss.

After the game and after all the celebrations had ended, I started walking across the field back toward the locker room, with the Island Cup in my possession. Before I left the game field, I saw Jacob along with his family. Jacob called me over and asked to have a picture taken together. I happily agreed. Later, I was told by Jacob's mother that Jacob had made that photo his Facebook profile picture.

I have several stories of individual achievements over the course of my career. I can honestly say that this story is one that I hold dear to my heart. Jacob told me that I had taught him a valuable lesson, one that he will always remember and cherish.

CHAPTER 24

"Whatever the mind of man can conceive and believe, it can achieve." — *Napoleon Hill*

Sometime in early 1983 I decided to grow a mustache after being clean shaven all my life. Maybe it was the influence of *Magnum P.I.*, the television show starring Tom Selleck. Perhaps it was because my upper lip was thin. All I know is my mustache has become an identifying feature and personal trademark. Since that first mustache, I offered to shave it off on three occasions.

In the beginning of my second year of coaching football at Martha's Vineyard, we were 4-0. Our next opponent was a league game with Bristol-Plymouth (BP), also 4-0. The winner of that game would likely win our league and advance to the Super Bowl. MV had never played in a Super Bowl.

BP beat us that day, 14-7 after scoring their two touchdowns on big plays. Their first score came on an interception return for a touchdown. Their second score came on a long run by their talented QB. We had a chance to tie the game late in the fourth quarter but came up short on a critical fourth down play.

After the game I could see the disappointment in my players. There were some outstanding young men in that senior class and they were incredibly dedicated to football. In just two short years this senior class had managed to revitalize a dying football program. Looking for a way to keep this team driven and motivated and finish the season with as many wins as possible, I decided to offer my mustache as motivation. I told the team, "If we finish the season 9-1, I will shave my mustache."

I was not sure if it was that deal or the fact that I had such a motivated team, but no other game that year was close. We won those games by an average of more than twenty-eight points and finished the season 9-1. Our last win was at home over Nantucket. That win was also my first Island Cup victory. Those nine wins set an MV record for most victories in a season up to that time. At the end of the Nantucket game I walked over to the concession stand and shaved my mustache off, much to the satisfaction of that 1989 team. At the time I was thirty-one years old. When that mustache came off, I looked like I could still be in high school. I started to regrow the mustache right away.

In the 2003 season our team was talented and had all the makings of a championship team. We had size, speed, strength, leadership, experience, and most importantly, desire and coachability.

In week two a solid Westwood High School team beat us, and we were embarrassed about how poorly we played. Westwood went undefeated and won their Super Bowl in a division higher than ours. I once again offered my mustache as motivation. However, I raised the ante from the 1989 season. This time I made the bet that the 2003 team had to win our Super Bowl.

Our team made it to the Super Bowl. The game was postponed one week due to a significant snowstorm which made playing all the Super Bowl games impossible. The Vineyard was playing Manchester High School at Chelsea High School. Chelsea was close to Manchester, so it was like a home game for them.

Just before the end of the second quarter, we threw an interception which was returned for a touchdown. Manchester took a 14-7 lead into halftime. That deficit was only the second time all year that we would trail. The first, of course, was in our loss to Westwood.

There was a calmness in our locker room. Our players were confident in their ability to win the game. We started the third quarter receiving the kickoff and went on a long, sustained drive to tie the game.

It was a hard fought battle and Manchester kept it close. The game came down to MV stopping Manchester on a game-tying two point conversion with less than a minute to play. The final score was Martha's Vineyard 26-Manchester 24. We finished the season 12-1 and won the school's fifth Super Bowl in seven attempts.

As promised, I went into the locker room to meet the players who had brought shears and other shaving items with them. I shaved my mustache before an exuberant football team. Players recorded the event and again, I started growing the mustache back the next day.

The mustache story continued during the 2012 football season. We were just a better than average team that year. After the seventh game our record was 3-4 with four games remaining. We had two league games and two nonleague games, including a game with a much improved Nantucket team.

At practice after the last game, which we had lost, I offered my mustache as motivation. It was not possible that we would make the postseason, so I made the deal that if we finished 7-4, I would shave my mustache. The team was excited.

We reeled off three wins and headed into the Island Cup game at home. I did not know people were discussing the bet about my mustache on social media until the middle of the junior varsity game that morning.

I was talking with their AD, Chris Maury, who said, "I hope we can save you from shaving your mustache."

Indeed late in the game it looked as if my mustache was going to be spared. Nantucket was winning 26-14 with just 4:46 left in the game. The last time Nantucket beat MV was in 2002. The Nantucket sidelines and stands were anxiously anticipating the final 4:46 to start their long awaited celebration.

When I looked up at the scoreboard and saw the twelve point difference and the time, I asked Bill Belcher, my longtime assistant coach, "Bill, does the scoreboard look familiar? You think lightning can strike twice?"

His reply was simply, "We have them right where we want them, Coach."

The scene was the same as in the 1992 Island Cup game played on Nantucket. MV was losing by twelve points, 12-0 with 4:41 left in the game. We came back to beat Nantucket.

We forced Nantucket to punt and had a quick scoring drive to pull within five points. That particular drive covered sixty-five yards on seven plays.

The Vineyard defense stopped Nantucket on three downs forcing them to once again punt. Their punter had not had a good day kicking the ball. We had our return called and our deep returners up close to the line of scrimmage. As fate would have it, the one time we hoped to get a bad punt, their kid boomed one. It sailed over our returners' heads. We had to start what would have to be the game winning drive from our own twenty yard line.

That drive had an ominous beginning. We threw three incomplete passes and had a five yard penalty. It was fourth down and fifteen with under two minutes to play. Basically it was convert on fourth down or lose the game.

I called for one of our more reliable pass plays out of the shotgun. The center snapped the ball over my QB's head. Somehow my QB, senior Alec Tattersall, was able to run down the ball, keep his composure, and fire a strike to fellow senior, Brandon Watkins. The result was a seventeen yard gain and a first down. We had new life.

Taking advantage of Nantucket's secondary mistake, we marched down the field and scored the eventual go-ahead touchdown with less than thirty seconds remaining in the game. They were using a man-to-man defense. When we sent a receiver in motion, instead of covering the motion man, that DB came on a blitz off the edge. The result was the motion man was left uncovered. We noticed this error in coverage when we sent our best slot receiver in motion from left to right. However, we threw from where the motion left. When nobody ran with the motion man or switched to cover him, we ran the same play but the second time threw to a wide open receiver. Our receiver caught the ball inside the five yard line and walked in, untouched, for the game winning score.

The Vineyard won the game 28-26 and finished the year at 7-4. On a side note, our quarterback Alec Tattersall, was written up in *Sports, Illustrated,* "Faces in the Crowd" column as a result of his performance in that game.

The scene after the game that afternoon was insane. People in the stands emptied onto the game field and everyone was celebrating. I had family fly up from Georgia for the game. My brother, Bobby, his two sons, Doug and Sam along with Sam's son, Trace, made the trip. They, too, ran onto the field. Bobby commented, "Man, I've never witnessed a high school football game this exciting." Pam and my children also came down onto the field to congratulate and celebrate with me.

Now, as promised, once back in the locker room I began the chore of shaving off my mustache. Players brought in clippers. I shaved in front of a bathroom mirror as the team watched, recorded, and cheered.

One player stated, "Coach, your mustache is going to break my shears. Man! That thing is thick."

I didn't know my mustache was such an iconic feature. Once I announced that the 2015 season was going to be my last, one of my former players, Peter Lambos (Class of 1998), designed a t-shirt.

On the front of the white t-shirt was purple ink. The ink formed a baseball cap, my face, and of course the mustache. The saying on the front of the shirt read, "Respect the Stache."

I always looked for ways to inspire and motivate my teams to play over and above their abilities. Maybe I should have offered to shave my mustache more often.

CHAPTER 25

"I make my practices real hard because if a player is a quitter, I want him to quit in practice, not a game." - Bear Bryant

Players hated the *terrible twenties*. They were performed when we played poorly and/or lost. In more recent years when a player forgot a part of his game day apparel or misbehaved, he also ran the *terrible twenties*.

What were the *terrible twenties*? The team was divided into two groups and each group went to opposite goal lines. At one end of the field the players performed twenty push-ups, while at the opposite end of the field the players performed twenty sit-ups, each rep to a coach's cadence. After those were performed to the coach's liking, the players jumped up and ran the 100 yards to the opposite goal line. Once there they performed the opposite exercise, nineteen push-ups or nineteen sit-ups, got up and ran the 100 yards to the opposite goal line. If anyone improperly performed a push-up or sit-up, the coach would have the entire group repeat that rep. This conditioning drill was finished once all players had worked their way down to zero. The drill took about twenty minutes or so to complete. Initially, I started having my teams do the *terrible twenties* if we lost a game. If we lost but played hard, we did the *teensy tens*, which started with ten push-ups or sit-ups and worked down to zero.

In 1993 we were coming off of back-to-back Mayflower League Championships and back-to-back Super Bowl wins. Our record in those two years was a combined 21-2. Our school's enrollment was starting to increase, as was the participation in the football program. Heading into the 1993 season I knew we weren't going to be as talented as the past two season's teams, but I thought we could still be competitive. Our team's success would be greatly determined by our off-season conditioning program.

I was disappointed in the team's commitment to the off-season program. On that first day of practice I wanted to send the message that I was not pleased with them.

We performed our conditioning test at the beginning of practice. Players were informed of the test weeks in advance. In one minute the players performed as many push-ups as they could, followed by one minute of maximum sit-ups. A timed twenty yard shuttle run and a timed two mile run completed the conditioning test. The two mile run was to be performed according to the player's offensive position and size. Failure to have a qualifying time would place the athlete in the *breakfast club*. Members of the *breakfast club* had to report at 6:00 a.m. each morning for a 6:30 practice start time and run the two miles until he made his qualifying time. This happened each morning in the first week of practice.

As usual, we had several players qualify for the *breakfast club*. After the two mile run, and after a ten minute water break, I then had the team run the *terrible twenties.*

Positioning myself at midfield so that I could see both groups, we were in the tenth sprint as senior offensive lineman, Kris Edwards, approached me. Kris was a short but rather large lineman. We all could tell he was struggling with the day's running.

As Kris neared, he stopped, walked up to me, shook my hand, and said, "Thank you, coach. I quit coach."

I started laughing and told him, "You're not quitting anything. Get your butt going and finish."

Kris, once again said, "Thank you, Coach," and finished.

I had more confidence in Kris finishing the run than he had in himself. That '93 team finished 7-3 and missed a three-peat by just two points. Our in-season conditioning played a major role in the team's success. From time to time, I see Kris and we have a good laugh when we talk about that first practice.

In 1995 the football team was returning from a difficult loss. We were defeated by an inspired Tri-County team 11-8. We fumbled what could have been the winning touchdown on the two yard line near the end of the game. That was the first and only time Tri-County defeated the Vineyard in football. We were young and inexperienced, basically a glorified junior varsity team, as we played several sophomores. This loss gave the Vineyard a 2 win and 6 loss record with two games remaining.

Because the game was played on Halloween weekend, I had instructed the team to behave themselves and reminded them if any team members became involved with any Halloween shenanigans, they would be disciplined with extreme measures. Unfortunately two juniors failed to heed my warning. They were caught throwing eggs at cars and at people, a bizarre Halloween tradition on the Vineyard.

The first day back at school that week also presented itself with some other disciplinary issues. Two other junior football players got into a fight with each other. Taking both incidents into consideration, I decided it was time to make an example out of those four players. Some AA—attitude adjustment—was needed.

After consulting with Jay Schofield and asking him for suggestions as to what discipline to hand out, I decided on a combination of both his and my punishments. Since the team had lost the previous weekend, they were scheduled to run the *terrible twenties* at the next practice. Jay suggested that while the team ran, the four guilty players should watch. I took it up a couple of notches.

On that overcast day I brought four lounge chairs, four cans of diet soda, and four Snickers candy bars out to the practice field. While I had the team run the *terrible twenties* in full pads, I told the four pinheads to enjoy their soda and candy bar while sitting comfortably in their own lounge chair. As if that wasn't enough, I also told the four players, "The more noise you make, the more you make fun of and laugh at your teammates, the less the team will have to run." Keep in mind the only players that knew what was going on were the four players being punished.

You can only imagine the scene that day. There were fifty-five or so athletes running this dreaded conditioning drill while four of their teammates were in lounge chairs, drinking sodas, eating candy bars, and making fun of them. On one occasion a player was upset at the fun being made of him. After the seventh or eighth sprint, when he was running back to his goal line, he decided to break off and run straight for the four boys in the lounge chairs. Fortunately for the four boys, a coach stopped the angry player before he reached them. At that point I decided enough was enough and I gathered the team together and explained the scene. I then gave the team a much deserved water break and cooling down period.

Later that practice, while doing a defensive scout drill, I assigned the same four boys to be offensive scout players for the upcoming opponent. We conducted this drill at our tire station. The offensive skilled players ran the opposing team's offensive plays while the defense made their adjustments and recognition. We normally didn't have contact during this drill, as there weren't any offensive linemen, but on that day that was not the case.

I picked the players who were being disciplined to represent four of the opponent's skilled players to run plays against our starting defense. I played quarterback. I made the drill full contact. After three or four plays with those four players getting hit, I stopped the live contact piece.

All in all, no one was hurt and those four young men learned a strong lesson. They learned that in order to be part of a team, they must put their personal wishes and goals on hold. Being part of a team is a full-time commitment. I see one of those four players from time to time and he still thanks me for that long day of practice his junior year.

The purpose of using such an intense discipline was to reinforce that playing football for Martha's Vineyard requires, among other things, self-discipline. When you play Vineyard football, the actions of one has an impact on all.

Another time I enforced the *terrible twenties*, for something other than a poor game, was in 1996. We were playing a nonleague game at Nauset Regional High School. This was Nauset's first year of playing a full varsity football schedule.

My coaches and I were talking at midfield after the junior varsity game. The varsity game was due to start an hour after the junior varsity game had finished. I looked toward the locker room and saw one of my starters, Asil Cash (who by the way, was a son of our school superintendent), jogging toward us. Asil was wearing all of his game uniform minus his white game jersey.

Once Asil arrived where we were standing, he told me, "Coach, we have a problem."

Naturally, I asked Asil, "What's our problem?"

Asil then said, "Coach, my mom forgot to pack my game jersey."

Immediately, I told Asil, "If you don't have your game jersey, you're not playing." I then said, "Don't ever let me hear you say that your *mom* forgot to pack your jersey." Asil, dejected, walked back to the locker room, changed into his travel clothes, and cheered his teammates on to an easy win. Even though our team won, Asil ran his *terrible twenties* that following Monday.

In 1999 a new way of doing the *terrible twenties* was established. When the Vineyard football team traveled, we often played a junior varsity game prior to the varsity game. This happened one Friday night in Weston, Massachusetts.

At the start of the '99 season I reminded the team that if anybody forgot any of their own equipment or game uniform, they would not play. I wanted to teach the players some responsibility; therefore, if a player forgot something needed for the game, they would not dress. There would be no debating, no matter who it was.

Early in my career I was given a great piece of coaching advice by Roosevelt Coleman. Roosevelt was a former head coach in Savannah and an assistant coach of mine.

His advice was, "Never have a rule that you cannot get out of. Never back yourself into a corner." I have tried keeping this piece of advice in mind throughout my career and was about to be put to the test.

We played Weston High School on Martha's Vineyard in November of 1998. We had played them the two previous years and had split the wins and losses in close contests. Our two schools were evenly matched. However, in 1998 I missed my first and only football game as a coach. Sadly, my mother passed away on November 2, 1998, in my home town. I was in Savannah attending her funeral and burial.

Weston came to Martha's Vineyard that Saturday and beat us rather easily 29-0. They had a good team, but I felt they were not twenty-nine points better than we were. I knew that we would be playing them in 1999, so I started making plans for that rematch as soon as our season ended.

On a cold Friday night in November of 1999, we were undefeated and playing at Weston. My junior varsity team was finishing their game, and my assistant coaches and varsity players were in the locker room getting prepared for our 7:00 kickoff. Players were getting taped and were in their own worlds. They were getting mentally prepared for a rematch that I had been looking forward to for one full year. Being dressed and ready to go outside, mother nature made its final pregame call to me. The bathroom was in the locker room where the other coaches were dressing.

Just when I was about to come out, I heard three players approach the coaches and ask them if they knew where I was. When the coaches told them that I was not inside, the players began to inform them that they brought the wrong game jersey or had forgotten it completely. They asked the coaches what they should do. Two of those players were starters and the other played on special teams and was a backup. Neither the players nor coaches knew that I could hear the entire conversation.

You can imagine what was going through my mind. Here it is one year after my mother's funeral, playing against the team I missed the previous year, and playing against the team that beat us rather easily last year. We were undefeated and I had this dumbass rule that I created. My own rule was going to prevent three good players from playing in what was probably the toughest game remaining in the season.

Then I remembered that great piece of advice. Now it was up to me to come up with an out. I needed to figure out a significant punishment but also appear as if I was not caving into the players' forgetfulness, all the while remaining steadfast to my principles.

Truthfully I was taking more time than necessary to complete my routine, due to thinking of a way out for these kids. All of a sudden it came to me. I guess you really can do your best thinking while on the throne.

Calmly I walked out of the bathroom, surprising the three players. When they saw me they immediately started babbling about how they brought the wrong jersey. Two of the players brought their practice jersey, same color as our away game jersey. The third player had just forgotten to pack his white game jersey. I asked them to explain our policy about forgetting game gear. They each said that they would not dress and began to hang their heads. One player even had to choke back tears.

After hearing all of their excuses, I told them that I had an alternative punishment for them. They were offered an out. I would let them dress and play by borrowing a junior varsity player's game jersey once their game was over. However, I informed them that by doing so, they were to bring their equipment bag to practice on Monday. At first they thought I was kicking them off the team. I told them that they were going to run the *terrible twenties* while carrying their equipment bag loaded with rocks. Without hesitation all three players enthusiastically agreed to the deal.

We went on to win the game that cold Friday night in Weston. The game was a back and forth contest. Trailing by five points in the fourth quarter, we converted on a crucial fourth down and ten from our own fifteen yard line late in the game. That conversion enabled us to drive the length of the field and score the go-ahead points to maintain our perfect season and eventually win our fourth Mayflower League and Super Bowl titles.

All three of those players made positive contributions in the win. They also carried a heavy load of rocks in their equipment bag on Monday while performing the *terrible twenties*. A new tradition had begun.

After that experience I created an equipment check list. This consisted of items to bring to away games. Each player was given a list before the first away game.

As coaches, we are often confronted with decisions that impact a player's growth. Oftentimes we refer to these opportunities as teachable moments. In three of the cases in this story, players messed up, but by staying committed to our principles and philosophies, they also learned a valuable life lesson.

The *terrible twenties* remained a staple of our conditioning drills. We continued running them with and without rocks through my last year of coaching.

CHAPTER 26

"When nothing is going right, go left." - Anonymous

Traveling to away games from Martha's Vineyard can sometimes be challenging. What could possibly go wrong with a forty-five minute boat ride each way and a round-trip bus ride to our opponent's school?

For many years travel for away games comprised of two school buses for players and coaches. There was a separate bus for the cheerleaders and a twelve passenger van loaded with our equipment. That was for the physical transportation. What about weather concerns? Would the boats run in windy conditions? If the boats ran, what was the trip going to be like in rough seas? If the boat was canceled, especially on our return, what were our options?

Fortunately my teams were never stranded away from Martha's Vineyard. We always made it back to the Vineyard that same day or night. However, we did experience a few scary boat rides and unusual occurrences.

My first boat issue occurred on my first official away game in 1988. We were playing at Bristol Plymouth (BP) in Taunton, Massachusetts.

I required that the team report to the SSA (Steamship Authority), thirty minutes before the boat departure time. All were present except for two brothers. Eric, a senior, and his younger brother Matt, a sophomore, who were not at the boat dock. These were my two starting defensive tackles.

At the designated time the boat left the Vineyard for Woods Hole. We were going to play our first game without our starting defensive tackles.

One of my assistants, Dave Morris, made arrangements for the brothers to ride to the mainland on a friend's boat. However, the team bus was not going to wait for them. Once in Woods Hole they had to find transportation to BP.

The cheerleading coach, who kept a car in Woods Hole, volunteered to stay behind, wait for the boys and drive them to the game.

The brothers eventually arrived at BP after the game had started. I allowed them to play that day but disciplined them the next week at practice. We lost the game 27-14.

The example I made of the brothers that next week got the attention of the rest of the team. I had them mow and rake the game field before they were allowed to play again. Unfortunately, that was not the last time a player missed the boat.

The next boat experience occurred on our return trip after winning our first Super Bowl in 1991. The team stopped and ate dinner at the Big Boy restaurant, located at the bottom of the Bourne Bridge in Bourne, Massachusetts. The Bourne Bridge is one of two bridges connecting the Cape and Islands.

As the team was preparing to load the buses for our twenty minute ride down to Woods Hole, the cheerleading coach asked me if one of her girls could ride to the boat on the football players bus. The girl had a boyfriend on the football team, Jason Dyer, our junior QB. I told her, "Absolutely not."

The junior varsity coaches, Bill Belcher and Dan Meader, were responsible for the players bus. The varsity coaches were not riding on the bus, as assistant coach Dave Morris made arrangements for the varsity coaches to return from the stadium in a limousine.

Before leaving the Big Boy, Bill did a head count while standing on the bus. It was dark out and the headcount was correct. We left the restaurant together with the school bus leading the way. The cheerleader bus was second in line followed by the limousine.

When we reached Woods Hole I received word that one of our players had been left behind at the Big Boy. An employee at the restaurant called the Steamship Authority to let us know that the player was being driven down to the boat by a State Police trooper.

Jason Tillman, a sophomore, was in the bathroom at the restaurant when the buses left. The head count was correct because the cheerleader did sneak onto the bus. Once the State Trooper delivered Jason, we all loaded the boat for our return trip. I had some harsh words for the cheerleader, as well as the cheerleading coach, and Jason Dyer.

Jason Dyer went on to be a three year starter at QB for us. He messed up plenty of times and that bus ride was not the first. He messed up so often that I gave him the nickname, Damn It Dyer. Jason and I are still close friends. He is listed in my cell phone contacts as Damn It Dyer.

Our next adventure with transportation occurred in 1992. We had a rare Friday afternoon league game at Blue Hills in Canton, Massachusetts. The boat and bus ride there went well.

We pulled up to the school and could see the field and noticed this grayish-white looking stuff covering the ground. From where we were nobody could tell what it was.

Once we were dressed and walked down to the field, it became evident what the grayish-white looking stuff was. It was goose poop. Little piles of goose poop littered the game surface. Everywhere we stepped there was a pile of this crap.

Being the away team, we wore white jerseys with white game pants. Before the game even started our players' uniforms were covered in goose poop.

We went on to win the game that day 28-0. After the game all the players put their game uniforms into their team bags and then loaded their bags into the equipment van. Dan Dyer, my QB's father, had volunteered to drive the van that day.

The team left Blue Hills together feeling good about the win. The bus arrived at Woods Hole, but the van was not with us. Keep in mind that this was long before cell phones. Contacting Dan about his location was not easy. We thought that he stopped for food before coming to the boat.

Nobody knew of his whereabouts.

Eventually I received notice at the SSA of Dan's location. The van had broken down in Holbrook, Massachusetts. Holbrook was still a good hour's drive away from the boat. The real problem was that it was after five o'clock on a Friday afternoon.

Dan had the van towed to a garage but nobody was there. Monday was going to be the first opportunity to fix the van. Dan was able to get to the boat and returned to the Vineyard with the team.

From Friday to Tuesday, the day the repaired van was returned to the Vineyard, the windows had not been opened. The van with all the team bags made it to school just in time for practice that Tuesday. You may be able to imagine the looks on the players' faces when I directed them to grab their bags, suit up and run onto the field for practice.

The next incident didn't have anything to do with transportation. It did; however, demonstrate the limitations that some islanders experience while growing up and rarely leaving the Vineyard. Our 1993 football season started with a Saturday afternoon away game at Ipswich High School in Ipswich, Massachusetts. Ipswich beat us 6-0 in 1992, our only loss that season. Ipswich was far enough away that the team spent Friday night in a hotel near the school.

Upon check in one of my younger players, sophomore Keith, pointed at the glass doors in the lobby and asked, "Coach Herman, what is that?"

I looked in that direction but was confused. I said, "You mean the elevators?"

His response was, "Yes, I've never been in one."

I was shocked at this. I told Keith, "Go for a ride, it's free. Have a good time."

Sometimes I took for granted what our students were exposed to as they were growing up.

For the next several seasons we traveled with few issues.

In 1999 we installed lights at our game field. It was becoming evident that the majority of high schools were also installing lights and playing

Friday night games. We all became aware of the benefits of playing under the lights. Attendance at night games was almost tripled compared to Saturday afternoon games. Playing games at night created an upswing in community support and an increase in gate receipts for the school.

Friday night games allowed the team to have weekends off, giving seniors the chance to make college visits without missing school or practice. Plus, Friday night games are what high school football is all about. The increase in Friday night away games meant that the athletes were released early from school. The MVRHS school day ended at 2:05 p.m. Most of our Friday night away games resulted in a 12:35 p.m. dismissal time for the 1:15 p.m. boat. When athletes were dismissed from school, a school bus was available to take team members to the SSA. The bus parked at the back of the school near the gym and locker room exit. Those athletes who could not drive took the bus to the boat.

On one particular Friday early release day, unbeknownst to me, Tony Breth, one of my juniors, figured he had time to drive his car to his house before coming to the boat. He had forgotten to pack his receiver gloves.

The team arrived at the boat, but Tony was not there. The boat left as scheduled. I looked around the vessel for Tony. I asked several players if they had seen Tony get on the boat but nobody had.

Shortly after the boat left, I received a phone call from the school. Tony was in a car accident near his house. He lived on a dirt road and was traveling too fast for the road conditions. He spun out of control and hit a tree. His car was totaled. Tony was taken to the hospital by ambulance. Luckily nothing was wrong with him and he was released, but he did miss the game.

The next day I called Tony to check on him. After I double checked to make sure he was okay, I asked him, "How much did those gloves cost you?"

He told me, "Roughly $50."

I said, "Nope, those gloves cost you $5,000. Isn't that how much your totaled car was worth?"

We were just happy that Tony was able to walk away from his accident with no injuries. Tony would not miss any more time from football as a result of his accident.

I was fortunate to never get stuck off-island with my team overnight as a result of missing the boat or having one canceled due to weather conditions. I did; however, come close twice during two of my last three seasons.

The first of those was due to a longer than usual game against Brighton High School near Boston. Due to the high number of passes thrown and scoring from both teams, this game took almost three hours to complete. Both sides scored over forty points. Fortunately, we scored more than Brighton that night.

Because the game took so long to complete, I allowed our team to get on the bus dressed in their game uniforms. The team ran to the school bus after shaking hands with Brighton. We all knew it was going to be close making it back to Woods Hole in time to catch the last boat at 9:45 p.m. As fate would have it, we hit Friday night traffic leaving Boston. As a result, the reality of missing the last boat began to sink in.

However, there was a contingency plan. There is a small transportation company based in Falmouth. This company has a small boat called the *Patriot* which travels to the island in almost every condition. However, we had more people than the boat could hold. Plus, we had to charter the boat for a cost to the high school.

Once we confirmed the team was not going to make the last SSA boat, we made plans to take the *Patriot*. Our athletic director contacted one of the *Patriot* captains, and he met us at their dock in Falmouth.

Due to our numbers the *Patriot* had to make two trips to the Vineyard. On the first boat trip, I assigned the cheerleaders and the players who lived farthest away from where the boat was going to dock once on the island. I also assigned most of the coaches to the first boat. That left David Araujo, an assistant coach, close to twenty players, and me in Falmouth waiting for the second trip.

Because we had to leave Brighton in such a hurry, none of us had eaten since 1:00 that afternoon. While we had to wait the ninety minutes for the boat to return, we loaded the school bus and went to a McDonald's in Falmouth.

Just as in 1993 when one of my players had never been in an elevator, we discovered that one of our island-born players had never eaten a Big Mac. Because Kyle was a senior and lived close to where the *Patriot* was going to dock on the Vineyard, he stayed behind for the second trip.

All in all it was a good day for the team and Kyle. We won an exciting high scoring game and Kyle got to enjoy his first ever Big Mac.

The closest I ever came to being stranded and not making it back to the Vineyard after a game happened in my last year of coaching.

We had a league game at Bishop Stang in Dartmouth, Massachusetts. Bishop Stang was only a fifty minute bus ride away from Woods Hole, one of our shorter trips.

The concern first started in the third quarter of the game. We had a ninety minute lightning delay. Both teams cleared the field and were relaxing inside the gym. On two occasions we attempted to go back to the field only to be instructed to go back inside due to more lightning.

At one point the referees called both head coaches together to discuss options. I had talked with my AD and informed him that I preferred staying at Bishop Stang and finishing the game. My AD was okay with that decision. I did not want to leave and have to return the next day to finish the game. It was my responsibility to contact the *Patriot* and make arrangements for our return trip later that night. I started making calls while we were in the weather delay. Unfortunately nobody at the *Patriot* answered any of my calls.

Finally the bad weather moved on and we were able to go out and finish the game, which we lost.

On our bus ride back to Falmouth, I continued calling the *Patriot*. I made at least ten more calls and each time left a message for someone to please call me back. Nobody ever did.

I had the bus driver take us to the *Patriot* dock on the outside chance that they got one of my messages and were waiting for us. We pulled up to the slip and saw the *Patriot* boat, but it was not there because of me or my calls. It just so happened someone else needed an emergency ride to the Vineyard that night. The boat was there to take them over. Because we had taken just the varsity team that day, we were all able to fit on the *Patriot* and made it to the Vineyard in one trip. We arrived on Martha's Vineyard just after midnight but at least we all made it back.

Come to find out, all of my messages were received. The captain had fallen asleep and missed all of my calls. He didn't respond because he was bringing the other passengers over. He knew he was going to be able to take us also.

Such is life when you live on an island without roads, bridges or tunnels connecting you to the mainland. It is true that Islanders' lives revolve around the boat. All trips off-island are first organized and structured based on the boat schedule.

It can sometimes be an inconvenience living on the island without being able to come and go as you please. It is also one of the beautiful things about living on the island. The hustle and bustle of mainland living does not exist here. That is why living on Martha's Vineyard is so much about community. We all experience so many of the same things.

CHAPTER 27

"Make up your mind that no matter what comes your way, no matter how difficult, no matter how unfair, you will do more than simply survive. You will thrive in spite of it." — Joel Osteen

As the 2000 football season came to a close, both the junior varsity and varsity teams ended with convincing wins over Nantucket. The varsity finished with a 10-1 record, securing our third Mayflower League championship in four years, along with back to back Super Bowl appearances.

After the game with Nantucket the team had two weeks to prepare for the Super Bowl. Our opponent that year would be a powerful Bellingham High School team. We would play the game at Boston University on the first Saturday in December.

Our game with Nantucket is traditionally played the Saturday before Thanksgiving, while other schools play on the morning of Thanksgiving. As in years past, I gave the team the day before Thanksgiving, Thanksgiving, Friday, and Saturday off. The players and coaches began preparations for Bellingham on Sunday. Due to our low numbers, it was common practice to have all players in our program, junior varsity and their coaches, continue the season, usually as scout teams. Practice that Sunday went without a hitch.

Monday, however, was noticeably different because Chris Rebello missed practice. It was unusual for him to not be at practice, especially without me receiving notification that he would not be there.

Chris Rebello, thirty-seven, was a beloved husband, father, coach, and an accomplished actor. As a child, Chris got his start in acting playing Michael, the oldest son of Sheriff Brody in the famous movie, *Jaws.*

Chris was born and lived all his life on Martha's Vineyard. He held various jobs after graduating from Martha's Vineyard Regional High School in 1981. Following his high school years, he had become an island fixture known mostly as a youth sports coach. He married Lynn Wadsworth on June 29th, 1985, and became a father to three beautiful children: James, Ashley, and Joel.

Chris loved coaching. His leadership skills were best shown coaching sports ranging from hockey to softball to basketball. In 1999 I needed an assistant coach for our junior varsity football team. Knowing Chris from Little League baseball, I asked him if he would be interested in coaching football. After clearing this with his wife (as all smart coaches should do), he was on board.

The following season Chris was promoted to head freshman coach. David Rossi, a police officer in Edgartown, and Karl Buder, owner of the Thorncroft Inn in Vineyard Haven, assisted Chris.

Being a caring person, Chris became a great role model for the youth on Martha's Vineyard. He identified with kids in need. Chris would reach out to any athlete who might have been struggling with adversity, whether in sports, school, or at home. He made each of them his responsibility.

Early in the 2000 season, Chris had his freshman team together at the conclusion of one of our two-a-day sessions and was giving them a talk before releasing them for the night. Late in the day mosquitoes are prevalent on the Vineyard, especially at our practice field. Chris was standing in the middle of twenty-five or so ninth graders, wearing his trademark baseball cap, giving a final post practice talk, and highlighting what were likely the key points he wanted to stress from the day. Chris was talking in a serious tone.

One player, a freshman also named Chris, was staring intently at Coach Rebello as a mosquito was circling the coach's head. At the peak of the coach's talk, the young player stood up, walked with a sense of urgency up to his coach, and forcefully smacked the coach's hat off his head. It was hardly a likely event. Everyone was shocked and not a sound could be heard.

Chris Rebello bent down, dusted off his hat, and put it back on. He just stood there, with his hat now perched sideways on his head. Chris carried his trademark smirk as he stared at the player out the corner of his eye. All the players silently stared and waited for the coach's reaction. Coach Rebello calmly asked the freshman, "What the hell was that about?"

The young player, still standing next to his coach, merely remarked, "Got him for you coach. I got that mosquito."

Chris Rebello thanked the young freshman, shook his head, and continued with his talk as if nothing happened. Of course, assistants Rossi and Buder were bent over convulsing with laughter.

That was the kind of person Chris was. Not many adults would stand there and get hit in the face and not have something angry to say. Chris innately understood that the young player was just looking out for his coach, and in turn, the coach was looking out for his player.

Chris was a committed coach. One day, he showed up to practice early looking like the Jolly Green Giant. He was installing a lawn, hydroseeding the yard, when the machine blew up in his face. Hydroseed was all over Chris. It was late in the day and Chris had to decide whether to go home and shower, which would make him late to practice, or show up at practice with this green crap all over him.

Chris chose to come to practice with hydroseed coming out of his mouth, ears, and nose. Of course, he received a lot of ribbing from the coaching staff, but he was there and on time.

The first indication of Chris' dedication came early in the 1999 season. During our double sessions, it was customary for the coaches to partake in free coffee and doughnuts from a local business. Being the rookie coach, Chris was assigned the duty of picking up the coffee and doughnuts and bringing them thirty minutes before the start of the morning practice for the coaches to enjoy. We started practice at 6:30 a.m. Chris was scheduled to have the coffee and doughnuts there at 6:00. On Chris' first morning he came at 6:00 without the coffee and doughnuts, saying that he woke up late. I immediately sent him away to get the coaches food and drink. He did so without complaint and never missed another duty assignment.

The following season, in 2000, we were preparing for our Super Bowl. When Chris missed Monday's practice, I went home and called to check on him. Chris answered the phone and apologized for not contacting me, but said that he had not been feeling well and was home with flu-like symptoms. He promised to be at practice Tuesday ready to go. I told him to get better, have some chicken soup, which I refer to as Jewish penicillin, and that the team missed him.

Tuesday morning, November 29th was rainy and chilly. I happened to be walking by the front office during my planning period around 10:00 a.m. The personnel in the office called for me to come inside. As I walked in, Chris' wife Lynn, who worked in the front office, was being consoled. All those in the office at that time were emotional, but at the same time calm and professional. A phone call had come in that Chris had suffered a heart attack up-island, in Aquinnah, while hunting with friends. Aquinnah is the farthest location from the hospital on the island. The full extent of what happened was still not clear, other than the fact that Chris had experienced a heart attack and that emergency responders had been called. In Aquinnah cell phone service rarely works.

While Chris had been in the woods hunting, he needed to go to the bathroom. He told his buddies to go ahead that he would catch up to them. When Chris failed to show up, one of his friends went back to check on him. He found Chris lying on the ground, motionless. All desperate acts to revive Chris failed. By the time the call came in for the ambulance, Chris had passed. Chris Rebello had succumbed to a heart attack.

After hearing what had happened, David Rossi and I went to get James out of his class and brought him to the front office. Not knowing what to tell James, we said nothing about Chris. Lynn had already left to go home. Tragic news spreads quickly in a small community like Martha's Vineyard. The Rebello family is a highly respected and well-loved island family. That meant there were plenty of Rebello cousins and family friends in the school. By the time we arrived with James in the front office, word had begun to get out about Chris. Other students who knew the Rebello family began asking questions and before long the entire school had heard rumors about the tragedy.

David and I drove James to his house in David's police cruiser. The drive took ten minutes but seemed like an hour. During the trip, James kept asking us what was going on, but we did not want to be the ones to tell him.

"You have a family member who was taken to the hospital in an ambulance and we're taking you home to be with your family," I told James.

It did not take long for James to figure out that something terrible had happened to his father. That was one of the worst car rides I have ever experienced.

David tried to break the sadness and whispered to me, "Lynn has just lost her oldest child." That statement described Chris perfectly. Chris loved life and the people around him. At age thirty-seven, Chris still approached life with childlike enthusiasm.

By the time we arrived at the Rebello home, several family members and family friends were already there. Lynn stood on the porch and as James approached they ran to each other and hugged tightly. She did not have to say anything to James but did anyway. She told him that his father had suffered a heart attack and was gone. Lynn and Chris' other two children had already arrived at their house and were being consoled inside by grandparents, aunts, and uncles. Ashley, the jewel of the family, was in the seventh grade and Joel, Chris' shadow, was in the fourth grade. Both were students at the Oak Bluffs School.

I remember standing on the Rebello front porch as friends and family were arriving. The yard, where cars could park, was full. There were a number of cars parked along the road leading to the Rebello home. As Lynn walked by me to go inside, she stopped, hugged me, and thanked me for allowing Chris the opportunity to coach football. The time Chris spent with James was precious. I hugged Lynn back and thanked her for letting us spend time with Chris.

This was now family time, so David and I drove back to the high school. On the way back, our conversation turned to our approach with our athletes. I asked David, "What are we going to tell the team? What about football practice that day?" After all, in four days we were to play Bellingham in the Super Bowl. Or would we? I remarked to David, "Today's events were not in the coach's manual or part of my contract."

Peg Regan, in her second year as principal at MVRHS, had made arrangements for me to meet with the football team upon my arrival back at school. An announcement was made over the school intercom for all football players to be excused from class and to go to the Performing Arts Center immediately. That would be the toughest meeting I would ever have with a group of young men.

My emotions were fragile. How was I going to maintain my composure while telling seventy or so 14-18 year olds that their thirty-seven year old coach and friend had just died of a heart attack? Fortunately for me, other staff coaches who were in the building, along with Mrs. Regan, were in attendance. Rumors had already started to surface as to what had happened, so I thought the first thing that needed to be said was to inform the team of the events as we knew them to be.

Michael McCarthy, assistant coach and head of guidance at our school, addressed the team and offered grief counseling to anyone who needed it. As expected, several players and staff began to cry, myself included. For so many, Chris was more than just a coach. For some, he was a father figure, a role model, a friend, and someone they highly respected. Now he was gone.

Players and coaches were allowed to remain in the PAC for as long as they needed. Most went back to class. Some went to the guidance office. As the school day came to a close, some four hours after the news, it was time for practice.

How does one practice after experiencing what our school and students had gone through, just four hours before? The question became, "Would we or should we even compete on Saturday?"

Robin Meader, Chris' older sister, had requested to meet with the team at the end of school that day. We met in the cafeteria. For someone who had just lost her baby brother, she was incredibly calm and collected. She explained what had happened to Chris and that when they found him, he had a smile on his face. Chris, possibly realizing what was happening, probably blurted out one of his favorite comments, "Oh, blega," Portuguese for "dick." Robin made sure that the team knew that their family wanted us to compete Saturday in the Super Bowl. Chris would not want it any other way.

The rest of that week was a blur. We prepared as best we could for an outstanding football team. The local media covered the story all week. Camera crews from Boston news stations flew in to interview us about the upcoming game. All we wanted to do was to be together and prepare for an emotional football game, one that we were dedicating to Chris and his family.

Friday came and, as in years past, the football team left school in the morning. We drove to where we would play, walked the game field, practiced at a local school, and stayed overnight in a hotel.

We had played at Boston University, BU, the previous year, so most of us had already seen the field. This year was about the team being together. When we arrived at BU, we went to the fifty yard line and said a prayer for Chris and his family. Remember, James, his oldest son, was with us.

It's now Saturday, game day. We happened to draw the first game time at BU, which meant a 9:00 a.m. kickoff. There would be more games played after ours that cold day. The temperature at kickoff was a balmy twenty-five degrees. There were areas of ice on the artificial turf. Before kickoff and before we would start our team pregame routine, we met once again at the fifty yard line to make a dedication to Chris. The players placed a large memorial with Chris' picture at midfield. It was facing our end of the field so that our players would see that Chris was watching over them in warm-ups.

It was time for the coin toss. I decided to have James walk out for the coin toss as an honorary captain. He was nervous, but we won the toss and opted to receive the ball. The team felt as if Chris was already taking care of us.

Bellingham kicked off and senior Travis Baptiste received the ball at our ten yard line. We executed our middle return and Travis hit the wedge at full speed. Travis raced ninety yards untouched for a touchdown and a six point lead. It was appropriate for Travis to score as he was close to Chris and had taken his passing hard.

Unfortunately, that would be all the scoring the Vineyard would do that day. We should have taken our ball and gone home after the opening kickoff return. We started off with a bang, but things went downhill fast. Jeff Lynch, one of our captains, a three year starter and two-way player, broke his ankle early in the first quarter. He assumed the leadership role in that game, making sure that all the players played their hearts out for Chris.

With Jeff now unable to continue, we lost to a talented and well coached Bellingham team. We didn't just lose, we lost big that day, our first Super Bowl loss. We had won our first four Super Bowls.

Toward the end of the contest, with the outcome already decided, I inserted James into the game. Freshmen rarely play for us in a Super Bowl, although Ben Gunn had started as a freshman the year before. James was hesitant to go into the game. He was afraid that he would make a mistake. I told him, "You're playing. There's no way in hell you're going to stand on the sidelines for this game." I patted him on the back, put him in the game at fullback and reminded him what to do.

The crowd from both schools responded with loud cheers as James went into our huddle. We ran the play and James did a great job of blocking their defensive end. He stayed in the game for that series, then it was over.

Three years later James and the other freshmen on Chris' team were seniors. James was one of the best players on the team, playing inside linebacker and tight end. That senior class was on a mission. They wanted to go out as Super Bowl Champions. One of their season goals was to shut out the league, not allow any points to Mayflower League teams. Coached by Bill Belcher, Dan Rossi, Steve McCarthy, Steve Barbee, and Mike McCarthy, long time assistants, they nearly did just that. The only league team to score on us that year was Nantucket. With the game already decided, they scored late in the game. We were back in the playoffs. It had been two years since MV was in the postseason, after losing to Marian High School in 2001.

In the 2003 postseason we played a solid East Boston team in the semi-finals, once again in frigid conditions. We played the game on artificial turf that had areas of ice on it. It was so cold that the water in our water bottles froze. The tops to the water coolers froze so that we could not open them. With the wind chill, the temperature during game time was a negative five degrees.

However, we won the game 17-15 to advance to the Super Bowl vs. Manchester High School. We were back in the Super Bowl, but had to wait an extra week to play due to a snowstorm. Some people felt that Chris Rebello was watching over us in this Super Bowl game and provided some divine intervention. With the Vineyard ahead 26-24 and under thirty-seconds to play, Manchester was going for a two point conversion to tie the game and possibly send it into overtime. Their QB threw a pass to an open receiver in the end zone, but the usually sure-handed receiver dropped the ball.

Each year we've won the Super Bowl, the players were awarded Super Bowl rings purchased by our Touchdown Club. Traditionally, the seniors design their rings. This year was no different. Except that year's ring would have the following engraved on the inside: C.R. Mission Accomplished.

The 2003 football team finished 12-1, dominated the Mayflower League outscoring those schools 181-7, and won the school's fifth Super Bowl title in seven attempts. More importantly, they accomplished their number one goal. This group of seniors had suffered a tragic loss as freshmen but stayed the course and finished their careers in a way that would have made their freshman coach, Chris Rebello, proud.

James Rebello made the Mayflower League All-Star team, the Cape Cod Times All-Star team, the Boston Globe All-Division team, and was selected to play in the Shriners Football game (the North vs. South Senior game). James attended Springfield College in Springfield, Massachusetts his freshman year of college, and played one year before giving up football and transferring to the University of Massachusetts, Amherst.

After the 2000 season, the football program would continue to honor the memory of Chris Rebello by establishing the Chris Rebello Memorial Award to be presented at our year end banquet. The coaching staff selected the recipient who best exemplified a player who had overcome adversity while playing football and one whom Chris would have nurtured. The player chosen receives his own personal plaque in addition to having his name engraved on the memorial plaque. The memorial plaque will always be on display in the school's trophy case area.

To this day, the Rebello family has a special place in the hearts of all islanders. The community and the football family informally adopted Chris' family on Martha's Vineyard.

Each year, at the end of the season banquet, I would ask Coach Bill Belcher, if he would like to present the Chris Rebello Memorial Award. Each year Bill would refuse because he knew that he would get too emotional.

Bill would tell me, "Donald, I can't do that. I know I will start crying and I don't want people seeing me do that."

That is how we all feel about Chris, even to this day. He will not be forgotten.

CHAPTER 28

"If you are afraid of confrontation, you are not going to do very well." - Bill Parcells

Martha's Vineyard is not alone when it comes to having issues with teen alcohol or drug usage. This is an ever-growing nationwide epidemic. When I started coaching on Martha's Vineyard, I wanted to ensure that my players were alcohol and drug free. I had been told teams in the past could not make that claim.

Something needed to be done. That was part of a conversation my coaches and I had during an off-season meeting back in the spring of 1994. My coaching staff that year consisted of John Bacheller, Dave Maddox, David Morris, Dan Meader, and Bill Belcher. We were contemplating starting a player contract for the upcoming season. Players and parents would sign the contract agreeing to the terms therein.

One of the most significant parts was a zero tolerance rule stating, "There is to be absolutely no drinking of alcohol, smoking, or other use of illegal substances. If a player is caught using or in possession of these substances, and violating this rule is confirmed by school officials, they will be terminated from the team."

There were several other rules included in that first contract but this one has drawn the most attention over the years. I don't want you to think that the Vineyard had a bunch of alcoholics and drug users playing football. The staff that year was trying to provide the healthiest environment we could to the teens on the Vineyard who were playing football. That contract was a first for Vineyard athletics. No other team had ever had such a policy or contract. In fact, the first season of the contract, after our fourth game, that rule was tested. One of our varsity starters violated the alcohol clause.

The young man came to me, of his own free will, and informed me that he had been caught by the police while in possession of beer. Once school personnel confirmed the incident, I removed the player from the team for the remainder of that season. He was extended the opportunity to come back the following year, his senior year, but chose not to return. Coincidentally, he is the only player to violate that rule, be removed from the team, and not return the following year.

One of the main reasons for establishing the zero tolerance policy was to give kids an out. The fact is we all know how strong peer pressure can be. If we could give a teenager an excuse to stand up to peer pressure and still be accepted, we needed to do just that. My players and their parents understood that this rule provided the player an out. They could refuse to partake in risky behavior because of something important to lose. I also told the players that if their friends were indeed their friends, they would understand this rule and not pressure them to break it.

Our school followed the Massachusetts Interscholastic Athletic Association, MIAA, Policy. There is a chemical health policy in place with the MIAA. We just went a step farther.

Over the years the MIAA tried to take a stronger stance when it came to chemical health and its violators. The MIAA Chemical Health policy used to read that a first time violator would face a two week or two game suspension, whichever was greater. Second time offenders of that policy faced stiffer punishment.

While this was a good policy for most, it was not strong enough for our program. We were looking for stiffer consequences. I realized that by taking a stronger stance, we ran the increased risk of losing starters and players every weekend. However, this was a position we thought was worth taking. After all, the last time I checked, drinking and use of drugs by high school age people was illegal and punishable by law.

In 1995 we had another alcohol violation. Another junior starter dropped several passes and kicks during a home game. The rumor was that he had gone out after our curfew calls the night before and had gotten drunk. As a result I asked our athletic director, Russ MacDonald, to call the player's mother in for a meeting to address this rumor. During that meeting the mother accidentally admitted that her son had gone out and had a few drinks. That was all the confirmation we needed. He was removed from the team but did come back for his senior year and made the league's All-Star team.

The next season also presented itself with another alcohol violation. This time another junior player came to my house late one Sunday afternoon. He told me that after he drove his car into a tree, the police were called that Saturday night and found several empty bottles and unopened beer in his car. The school confirmed this with the police and that players season came to an end.

Due to the dangerous incident involving drinking and driving, I decided to have a parent-coach meeting Tuesday night the following week. Most parents showed up and the violation was discussed. My goal was to have parents start holding their kids accountable for their actions and for them to start being accountable to each other. At this meeting a parent raised his hand and asked a question that to this day is still a head-scratcher.

The parent stated how much all the parents appreciated what we, as coaches, did for their sons on Friday nights. He then asked, "Was there any chance you could do something for them on Saturday nights as well?"

My first response was, "If I did, my wife would probably divorce me." My next response was simply, "No, Saturday nights are when you have to be parents."

That year was also the first time that the Touchdown Club sponsored Friday night dinners and a movie for the football team. Back then the team played on Saturday afternoons. Friday's practice had a late start time, 4:00 p.m. The late start allowed players time to get extra help from teachers, get haircuts, and watch other fall sports teams play. We practiced from 4:00 to 5:30 p.m. At 6:00 p.m. all players reported to the cafeteria for a pasta dinner. After the dinner the team would then watch a movie, usually football related.

Players were released from the cafeteria between 8:30 and 9:00 p.m. Coaches would then begin making phone calls to players' houses at 10:00 p.m. Each coach had his list of players to call, and it was at the discretion of the coach just how many and whom he would contact.

The two requirements that the coach had were to talk directly to the player and only use landlines, no cell phones were allowed. If a player was not home for his phone call, he did not dress the next day in the game. This practice continued until I retired.

The next couple of years or so went on without any incident regarding the chemical health policy. We thought we were making some real headway, either that or the kids were just better at not getting caught.

Then came the 2000 season. That season would eventually go down as another season from hell (at least for me). We were coming off an undefeated campaign in 1999. The prospects were good for us to repeat as league champs.

We had just finished our last preseason scrimmage on Labor Day weekend. The players had Saturday night and Sunday off. That Monday, Labor Day, started game week for us.

Sunday morning I received a call from a reliable source. He informed me that three players, all sophomores, were caught by the police Saturday night, found drinking or in possession of alcohol. Two of those sophomores were going to get varsity playing time, maybe even start.

After hearing about these accusations, I contacted all three players' parents and requested a meeting with them at school that Sunday. The players and at least one of their parents were in attendance. I asked the players to explain to me what had happened that Saturday night. They all confessed to violating the team's contract. I informed them about what had happened to other players over the years who had violated this policy. I told them that their season was over.

It has always been hard for me to end a high school athlete's season over a team rule's violation. Regardless, I knew that it was in the best interest of the student-athlete and that I had to be consistent in the enforcement of the policy. I have always felt that if you are going to have a policy, it must be enforced.

At the next practice I informed the rest of the team what had taken place over the weekend and that three players were removed from the team. Thankfully all of the players understood and supported the decision. That was the first time since this rule was established that more than one player had to be removed from the team.

I must go on the record stating that all of these kids were good kids. Teenagers will sometimes make stupid choices. Part of the education piece of being a coach and an educator is to help the athletes improve their decision-making. I firmly believe that if they know what the consequences of their actions are, the less likely they are to make those mistakes. At least that was my hope.

The last week of the regular season we were one win away winning our fifth Mayflower League championship. Monday night, the week of our game with Nantucket, two weeks before our eventual fifth Super Bowl, proved to be a special night. The school committee met.

Unbeknownst to my athletic director, Russ MacDonald, and to me, the school committee heard from the parents of one of the boys I removed from the team some twelve weeks earlier. The long and short of it was that the school committee voted to fully reinstate all three players onto the football team for the Island Cup game and the Super Bowl.

Tuesday morning, before my first-period class, the AD came into my office. He asked me if I had heard what had happened at the school committee meeting the night before? I told him, "No." He then informed me.

I am sure that most of you have seen cartoons with smoke coming out of a person's head. You now have a visual of what my reaction was to the news. I told my AD, "Bullshit! There's no way this is going to happen." He was visibly upset as well. Neither of us saw this coming or were told that this might be discussed at the meeting. Had we known, we both would have been there.

I was scheduled to teach a class that Tuesday morning before my first break. That was not going to happen that morning. I told my co-teacher, Lisa Knight, that I could not teach my class. I immediately went to the front office to talk with Principal Peg Regan.

It just so happened our Superintendent, Kriner Cash, walked into the front office as I was arriving. I had coached Kriners' three sons in football, so he was aware of our program and our policies.

Let's just say that we had a spirited conversation that morning. I asked the administration to please explain to me how this happened without the AD or me being present at the school committee meeting. I restated my position about the three student-athletes that there was no way they were playing football this season. We all came to an understanding that the boys would indeed, not play football that year.

During that off-season, my coaching principles and ethics were a hot topic and widely discussed in the Letters to the Editor section of the two island newspapers. One of the boy's father would publicly rake me over the coals for ruining his son's reputation. I refused to fight my battles in the paper; therefore, I did not respond to any of his accusations.

Another interesting thing took place that off-season. I received countless phone calls, emails, and letters of support, both private and public, from people from all over the country. While I can understand this particular father's stance involving his son, I had to look at the bigger picture.

Decisions had to be based on what I thought was best for all of my athletes and the football program. Unfortunately this father took it as a personal issue. I had nothing personal toward his son. He violated a team rule, broke the law, admitted to doing so, and was punished in a timely and consistent manner. Some parents just have to get over it.

Winter time on Martha's Vineyard can be slow. There aren't many exciting things happening here. So when anything newsworthy occurs, people tend to pay more attention. That was the case the winter of 2001 following the issues of the 2000 football season.

The school committee established a subcommittee to investigate a school-wide zero tolerance policy. They charged Principal Peg Regan to chair this committee of roughly twelve members. It was comprised of athletes, including one of the terminated players, high school teachers, coaches, parents, other community members, and me.

Keep in mind that the school committee was of the opinion that a zero tolerance policy would never happen. "The line has been drawn in the sand." That was a frequent quote from more than one school committee member. So when the subcommittee was established, I had hoped that a

147

zero tolerance policy would have a chance of being approved and implemented for the entire student body.

The subcommittee met several times during a three month period and would last between one to one and a half hours. Of course, the opinions of the students weighed heavily. At the end of the three month discussion period, Principal Regan decided that the topic had been exhausted and it was time for the subcommittee to vote. Much to my surprise and delight, the subcommittee voted unanimously to have a zero tolerance policy at Martha's Vineyard Regional High School.

After recording the last vote, Principal Regan announced her appreciation to the committee for the time and effort we all put in and stated, "I am going back to the school committee and informing them that the school will maintain the current MIAA Chemical Health Policy."

The line had been drawn in the sand.

The school committee met the first Monday of each month. At their next scheduled meeting, I was present to hear the report. The school committee voted on the motion to keep the Chemical Health policy for the school the same as the MIAA. I then raised my hand, was recognized by the chairperson, and given the right to speak. I told them how disappointed I was in this process and asked, "Head coach determines playing time, correct?"

One of the committee members actually asked, "What does that mean?"

That question may have caught the school committee off guard. They all agreed that they would not be involved with telling any coach who he or she has to play. I made sure this statement was on record and in the minutes of that meeting.

With that said, I thanked the school committee and informed them that I was enforcing my version of a zero tolerance policy. Instead of removing a player from the team, after confirmation of a violation, I would allow them the opportunity to remain on the team. However, they would not dress for any games for the remainder of that season. That was the football team's policy from the 2001 season until I retired in June of 2016.

And yes, we continued to have more violations. All of those players stayed in the program but did not dress for games. None of the violators quit. To me, that was a testament to the student-athletes and how they viewed being a part of our football program.

The second case of multiple violators occurred in 2003. This would also be the first time when the new policy would be put into effect; head coach determines playing time.

We had an away game at Weston High School on Friday night and were staying in a local hotel after the game. The next day we had plans to attend the Northeastern University college football game.

We beat Weston and stayed in Dedham, Massachusetts. After having all the players checked into their hotel rooms by 9:45 p.m., I told them I was taping them in at 10:30 p.m. I learned a neat trick from John Bacheller, former assistant coach, years earlier. John was an elementary school teacher and administrator, and often chaperoned overnight trips with his students.

In order to ensure that his students stayed in their rooms, John placed scotch tape on the outside of the room door. He placed the tape on the doorknob and on the door frame. It's impossible for the door, once opened, to be closed from the inside and have the tape stay in place. Using John's trick, I told the players that if any coach walked by their room in the morning and the tape was not in place, the season was over for all the players in that room.

I was in my hotel room along with other coaches, preparing to tape the players into their rooms when my hotel room phone rang. Assistant coaches Steve McCarthy and Steve Barbee were in the halls and called to have me report to a certain room. Assistant coach Michael McCarthy and I went to the room in question. I asked Steve McCarthy, "What's going on?"

He told me, "Just go inside the room."

That particular hotel room was set up with the bathroom door on your immediate left. The television was straight ahead and the two queen beds were also on the left. I opened the door, took two steps inside and by the time I got to the bathroom door, I had the munchies. I noticed a Visine tube on the entertainment center.

As I continued walking into the room, I said, "Jesus, what the hell were you idiots thinking?" I got beyond the bathroom and saw the four players, all junior varsity, sitting on their beds. Apparently they thought if they smoked in the bathroom and turned on the exhaust fan, the smoke and smell would disappear.

I asked for a show of hands for those who had been smoking. Three players raised a hand. I told those three to get up and come with me to my room.

Once in my room, the other coaches and I began blasting them for their conduct. Mike McCarthy, who was also the head of guidance at MVRHS, told the three, "We try to do something nice for the team and this is the thanks we get? You mean to tell me your habit is so bad, you couldn't miss one night of smoking that crap?"

After I had a turn with the three stooges, I instructed them to call home and tell their parents what had occurred, then I took the phone and explained what I wanted them to do. The next morning the team was leaving the hotel at 10:00 a.m. I insisted that each guilty player be picked up by a family member before we departed. I called a school official to inform them of what happened and what I was doing with them. Seeing as we live on the island, getting to Dedham by 10:00 a.m. was no easy task. Each family made arrangements to have a family member pick their child up on time.

As it so happened, instead of attending the college football game at Northeastern University, we went to Brockton High School where our boys' soccer team was playing in the state South Semi-Finals. Both of my sons were playing. Unfortunately the Vineyard soccer team lost in penalty kicks.

Upon the start of school the next Monday, each of the three boys received suspensions from school for misbehaving on a school sponsored field trip. I also suspended them from playing in any more football games that year. All three did continue being a part of the team by practicing the remainder of the season.

The following year presented itself with another trio of players suspended. On a Sunday afternoon, two juniors and a sophomore were riding in a car going to celebrate another player's birthday at the birthday boy's home.

I was told that a State Trooper had clocked the driver speeding at over 100 mph in a 45 mph zone. To make matters worse, as the trooper was in pursuit, he saw the boys throwing beer out of the driver's side windows, into oncoming traffic. The driver of the car was one of the boys suspended the year before for smoking in the hotel.

Once again I enforced the head coach determines playing time policy. As in the year before, all three boys remained with the team. Two of the players were varsity starters and the third a second stringer.

After the season one of the juniors told me that the hardest thing he had to do was sit there and watch his teammates play those games and not be able to contribute. He told me that he learned an important lesson. These were the last players I had to suspend for violating our chemical health policy.

I never took any enjoyment in enforcing this policy. I did, however, feel that it was something that separated our program from others. Our players knew the consequences. I don't know if the usage ever declined because of this policy. I do know that when a player had to watch their team compete from the sideline, it made an impact.

Being a part of a team often means putting your needs on hold. Being committed to a cause and to others is important in life. We tried to teach life skills while still putting the best team on the field.

Fortunately, we won many more games than we lost when we had to suspend players. But winning was not the most important thing to me. One of my primary goals was teaching young men the value of sacrifice and commitment.

CHAPTER 29

"Be more concerned with your character than your reputation, because your character is what you really are, while your reputation is merely what others think you are." - John Wooden

My good friend and one time colleague, Jay Schofield, once told me, "Your career is not complete unless you've been sued or accused of discrimination."

Thanks Jay, for I accomplished both. I guess my coaching and teaching career was complete.

After one of my players was injured during a practice, I was named in a lawsuit. The injury occurred during a football practice in which there were six coaches and an athletic trainer present. The player suffered a non-life-threatening injury to an internal organ.

That player left school at the conclusion of practice, along with the rest of the team, without saying a word to anyone that he was hurt. Later that night, complaining of stomach pain, he was taken to the hospital by his parents. He was hospitalized for several days and released. He did not return to football the rest of his high school career.

A few years after the initial injury, I was informed by my principal that I was named as a codefendant in a lawsuit. That player's family was suing the school for wrongful injury. Those parents accused me of allowing older players to repeatedly hit their son. Our school provided me with legal representation. I was summonsed to give a deposition, something I'd never done before, in Boston. Accompanying me that day was one of my junior varsity assistant coaches, Karl Buder. I never understood why Karl was asked to give a deposition. Karl was not on the varsity coaching staff but was present at practice that day. Karl's deposition lasted an hour and a half.

Mine, on the other hand, took over four hours. The deposition took place in an interview room at my lawyer's office. Present during my deposition was my lawyer, the plaintiff's lawyer, and a stenographer. Prior to starting, my lawyer had instructed me to give brief answers, one word answers when possible.

I can't tell you how many times the plaintiff's lawyer asked me, "What is a forearm shiver? Describe to me what that technique is."

I can only think that he was hoping I would make some sort of admission of guilt, or was he getting paid by the question?

I met with my lawyer or spoke with him by telephone several more times before we eventually went to trial.

Both sides had a professional witness. Mine was a current high school football coach and athletic director in Massachusetts. We had a controlled scrimmage with this coach's team a few years prior. He saw me in action with my team up close and personal. On the other side, the plaintiff's professional witness was a retired football coach from the 1950's. He was a much older coach and from a different state.

We had one brief day in court on Martha's Vineyard. I returned the morning of the second day ready to give my testimony. Before going into the courtroom, my lawyer brought me inside one of the rooms in the courthouse and informed me that the high school had just called him and was settling out of court.

I was furious. My lawyer told me that by settling, nothing would become record or precedent-setting. Also, settling was not an admission of guilt.

With the lawsuit over and behind me, I needed a discrimination case brought against me to make my career complete, according to Jay. Sure enough, that happened.

I have never not played someone based on their color or ethnicity. I believed in putting the players on the field who gave us the best chance to succeed. If an athlete worked hard and performed as coached, he played.

The only consideration I ever gave to playing one player over another was if one was a senior and the other younger. I gave the senior the first opportunity to start. However, if the senior was not getting the job done, I replaced him with the younger athlete.

This situation occurred at the midway point in one of our seasons. I started a senior over a younger player. The senior had been in our program all four years. He had seen varsity playing time as a junior and earned his varsity letter jacket. In his senior year I changed his offensive starting position to the backup role that he held the year before.

The senior was a minority and the younger player was not. After our second loss and at the midway point of the season, I told both players that I was reopening their position. I was not happy with the senior player's game performance. That week I informed both players that they would receive equal reps at their position during practice. I would take three days to decide who the starter was going to be for the upcoming weekend's game.

I decided to go with the younger player. The senior did, however, start on both sides of the ball. At the midway mark of the season our team was 3-2. After the change we would finish the second half of the season, arguably the tougher half, with a 5-1 record. I knew I made the right decision for what was best for the team.

The parent of the senior did not agree with my selection. He felt that color played a large part in my decision making. The parent went as far as to get the local NAACP involved.

At the conclusion of the season, the NAACP did their investigation. They had watched games and conducted interviews. Their finding was that no discrimination had taken place. Two of the three football team's captains that year were student athletes of color. That may have played a part in their findings.

Once the NAACP investigation finished and their findings were released, I informed Jay Schofield that my career was complete.

CHAPTER 30

"People who never dream, or never set goals, let life go by day by day letting others determine their destiny." - Catherine Pulsifer

The New Oxford American Dictionary defines tradition, in part as the transmission of customs or beliefs from generation to generation, or the fact of being passed on in this way. I've always believed traditions play a large part in the fabric of our society, especially in sports. You may have heard references to tradition by players, coaches, and announcers when a team was victorious. The first example of this is when you hear a football team's defense described as, "traditionally strong against the run." A second example is, "our university has a steeped tradition of excellence."

When I first arrived on the Vineyard, I asked people what the football program was known for and what traditions existed. I was looking to build on established traditions and wanted to create new ones. The tradition that I heard most was how aggressive and physical the Vineyard defense played. Being a defensive minded coach, that was one tradition I wanted to maintain. Some negative traditions were also mentioned. My mission became to change the culture in the football program and the community's perception of football on Martha's Vineyard.

Three of my primary goals were to create a parent booster club, a strength and conditioning program, and establish a respected program.

None of these were in place when I arrived in August of 1988.

Touchdown Club

My first week on the Vineyard, I organized what would eventually be known as the Martha's Vineyard Touchdown Club or simply, the TD Club. This organization became the football team's booster club.

I organized a meeting with parents of prospective players who were interested in starting the club. We organized ourselves and elected officers and began establishing ways to raise money to support the football team. The school's budget line for football, at that time, was $4,500. More money was needed to accomplish what I wanted.

From 1988 through my last season in 2015, the TD Club was the lifeline for the football program at MVRHS. The football budget line remained the same during my entire tenure. There was absolutely no way the football program could have accomplished the many things it did without the help and support of the TD Club.

One big misconception about football at MVRHS was the belief that the TD Club received all monies raised at home games. The TD Club gained little financial benefit from home games. The gate receipts went into the school's general fund. The money raised at the concession stand went to the junior class. The junior class manned the stand and put all funds raised toward their junior prom.

The only money raised by the TD Club at home games came from 50/50 raffles and the selling of programs and souvenirs. The club raised their money in many different ways.

One of the most successful, yearly fundraisers was the Purple Pride Card. The first two years, 1999 and 2000, the team did this through a national fundraising company. The money raised was a 50/50 split. Then David Rossi, an assistant coach and parent of a player, suggested that we create our own island version of the Purple Pride Card. He contacted local island businesses and had them agree to give discounts. David had several new businesses donate to the card. Maybe this happened because he wore his police uniform and gun when asking them to contribute. One example of the discounts offered on the back of the card was free appetizers with the purchase of two entrees at a local restaurant. Resembling a credit card, the TD Club logo was on the front, and there was a list of the contributing businesses and their discounts on the back. The school colors are purple and white; one year the card would be purple, the next year it would be white. We had between 12 and 15 contributing businesses and most of them would renew their offers each year. The card was good for one calendar year and cost $10.

I mentioned earlier that establishing a strength program was one of my top goals. One way we accomplished this was by holding a yearly Lift-a-Thon fundraiser. The Lift-a-Thon earned money by having the team do a bench press, one-rep max. Each player enlisted sponsors to donate money for each pound lifted while performing the bench press. Each player had to raise a minimum amount of money.

As an incentive to raise more money than what was required, we had prizes in place for those who raised the most money and benched the most weight. Those prizes varied from cleats to gift certificates at a local sporting goods store. They could also earn their *purple pride stripe.*

In addition to the Lift-a-Thon and Purple Pride Cards, the TD Club held an annual auction. The event usually took place on a Saturday night in November. Players and their families were asked to collect donated goods for the auction. During the auction I played the male version of Vanna White by walking down the aisle displaying the article up for sale.

In the mid-2000's the TD Club purchased a food booth for the annual Agriculture Fair, a four day event. The tempura booth became known for selling touchdown tempura; fried mixed vegetables. Members of the club manned the booth in which fair-goers purchased an order of tempura. Egg rolls and drinks were also available for purchase.

The Club conducted a couple of smaller fundraisers. They went from raising in the neighborhood of $10,000 in the early years to raising nearly $60,000 a year in later years.

On the years of home Island Cup games, the Club sponsored a spirit event. People would pay for a sign placed in the ground and would have various sayings written on them. One example was, "Keep the Cup." Another sign might say, "Good luck #53." These signs lined the road from the Steamship Authority to the high school. They were white signs with purple paint. These signs were positioned so that the visiting Nantucket team and their fans could see them on the ride from the SSA to the high school. Seeing those signs was an awesome sight. There were years when over 200 signs lined the three mile stretch of road.

We had several presidents of the Club in the early years. Jack Law joined the TD Club in 1994, and two years later became the TD Club president and remained in that position until he retired in June of 2016. Jack's daughter, Olivia, had been a team manager.

Another longtime TD Club officer was Denise Lambos. Denise had two sons who played football. Her oldest son, Peter, was a starter on the 1997 undefeated team. Denise's second son, Brian, started on the 1997 and 1999 teams. Both Peter and Brian were seniors when their teams went undefeated. Denise served from 1994 until June 2016 and was the Club's secretary and activity coordinator.

Even though the TD Club raised several thousand dollars each year, they also spent several thousand dollars each year. I provided most of the direction for the Club when it came to spending. The Club's money went to whatever the needs of the program were after the school's budget was spent.

The TD Club purchased player equipment, bought our practice and game uniforms, paid for practice field equipment, bought game day equipment such as headsets, down markers, and sideline markers. They purchased team equipment bags and coaches bags. When the original bleachers were condemned after the 1989 season, the Club assisted the school with funding and installing new bleachers.

When the scoreboard at the game field needed to be replaced, the TD Club stepped in and paid for the new one, even though football was not the only sport which used the scoreboard. The game field also serviced soccer and lacrosse, both boys' and girls' teams.

In 1999 the school installed lights at the game field. The TD Club provided the workforce for the installation and covered the cost difference between what was donated and what was needed. The Club also paid for the construction of the TD Club booth at the game field, which also doubled as the ticket booth. The school needed a new sign in front of the building to announce events. The TD Club contributed money toward the sign. The Club also donated an AED (automated external defibrillator) to the school.

The Club paid for the coaching staff to attend coaching clinics on a yearly basis. On a couple of occasions, my staff participated in a coaches' clinic at the United States Naval Academy, in Annapolis, Maryland. The Club paid for airfare, hotel, rental cars, and clinic registration fees.

Then of course, there were the numerous events the Club sponsored on behalf of the players themselves. We began having weekly team pasta dinners the night before our games. Before home Saturday afternoon games, the Club provided the team with breakfast. When we traveled, the Club paid for team sandwiches which came from an Island deli. The Club made sure we were well fed, especially the night before our rivalry game with Nantucket.

On those nights the Club grilled steaks for all team members. They invited various community members to be guests at the dinner. One year they invited members of the first MVRHS football team and cheerleaders on their fifty year reunion.

The Club provided money to purchase end-of-the-year awards. The school provided a small number of award plaques. Whatever other plaques were needed, the Club sponsored. Everyone involved in the program left the banquet with something from the Club.

Another yearly expense was varsity letter jackets. I determined who received these from the policy we established.

Whenever we won a Super Bowl, the Club bought each member a ring. Coaches, managers, cheerleaders, and anyone associated with the program received their Super Bowl ring at no cost to them.

Four graduating seniors who were continuing their education were eligible for a $1,000 scholarship. Each senior player received one piece of paper with their name on it for each year in the program. If they played all four years, they added one more slip. I was allowed to put four slips into the hat with anybody's name. The slips of paper went into a hat and four names were randomly drawn. Once the cheerleaders became a part of the Club, they received one $1,000 scholarship, selected in the same manner.

When we began playing Friday night games, I arranged for the team to attend college games. We attempted to do this once a year. The Club covered the cost for the bus and admission.

Then there was the homecoming dance and festivities. The Club paid for everything associated with the dance which included crowns, flowers, decorations, food, DJ, and the cost of the location when it was not held at the school.

Every year we held a Spirit Week the week of the Island Cup game. The week culminated with a bonfire pep rally on Thursday night. The Club took care of this as well as the coffin to be thrown into the fire. While the bonfire was happening, parents were inside the school decorating the cafeteria and locker rooms.

As I mentioned earlier, the club sponsored the cheerleaders and eventually, the junior high football team, our feeder program. They covered all the costs to run those programs when the school system fell short.

As you can easily see, without the TD Club, the experiences and opportunities made available to the members of the Vineyard football program would have never happened.

Strength and Conditioning

My second priority was establishing a strength and conditioning program. In 1988 Martha's Vineyard Regional High School did not have a weight room. In the off-season after my first year, the team lifted weights at a local gym. The gym charged players a minimal weekly fee. Three days a week players would find round trip transportation to that gym.

After my second season the school was provided a small space across the street from the high school in the Martha's Vineyard Community Service complex. That was the school's first official weight room. The TD Club purchased all the equipment.

The weight room at Community Services was on the floor underneath where counseling for battered women occurred. That location was not ideal, as you had teenage boys slamming weights and making lots of noise while women were being counseled.

Shortly after that we moved the weightlifting equipment into the loft above the automotive shop at the school. We remained there for several years.

Eventually we relocated the weight room into a metal building on school grounds. In 2005 the TD Club paid to renovate and fully equip the facility which we used until I retired. The school began buying some equipment, as the physical education classes and a few other sports teams also used this facility.

Having a strength and conditioning program was instrumental to our success. More times than not, we were the stronger and better conditioned team on the field. I know that by having these programs in place, our athletes suffered fewer injuries and recovered quicker when they were injured.

Respect

Having the TD Club established and a strength and conditioning program in place, I turned my focus to making our program respected, not only on Martha's Vineyard but across the state of Massachusetts. I tried creating various ways to motivate our players so that the students wanted to be a part of the football program.

In the mid-1980's, Don Lindsey, Georgia Tech's defensive coordinator under head coach Bill Curry, created the Black Watch defense. Defensive players earned their black stripe which was placed down the middle of their gold helmet. The stripe signified a great effort by that player in the previous game.

When I first came to Martha's Vineyard and saw the white helmets, I knew I wanted to start my version of the Black Watch. However, I did not limit the stripes to just defensive players. I made the award open to all team members and used a purple stripe. Hence, we started the Purple Pride Club.

After the coaches viewed the game film, we awarded the stripe to one or more players who had an outstanding performance. The coaches made player recommendations and the staff would vote. The winning player(s) received their purple stripe before the next game.

For many years I kept a large white poster on my office window. When a player received their stripe, I wrote their name in purple marker on the poster. The student body was able to see who earned their stripe.

The TD Club made space on a page in the program for recipients of the purple stripe. The player's picture appeared on the page dedicated to the Purple Pride Club. The purple stripe became a badge of honor.

As the seasons progressed, we decided on different ways players could earn their stripe. One was to reward players for their academic performance. I gave a list of players' names to the school guidance department. Usually Michael McCarthy, head of guidance, checked the GPA's from the previous school year and let me know which player had the highest GPA.

We also awarded stripes to the top lifter at our Lift-a-Thon.

In the mid-2000's the coaching staff realized some non-starting players were working hard in practice. Most of those players would not see enough playing time to earn a stripe. We decided to start awarding a Practice Player of the Week and issuing that player his stripe. It was amazing to see how many nonstarters began working harder in practice so that they could have a chance to receive their purple pride stripe. As a result, our scout teams became better which made our starters have to work harder. It was a win-win situation.

Team members could have their stripe taken away. Players who misbehaved in school or violated team policy would have their stripe removed. They could, however, earn it back.

Another way players became recognized for their game performance, was being awarded Player of the Week. The coaching staff would typically select four players from the previous game. These individuals would be recognized as top offensive player, defensive player, special teams player, and coaches' player. Each of these winners received a certificate for one free large pizza at the sponsoring location. There were times when the coaching staff did not feel anyone deserved an award, and none were given out for that category.

Another idea that I brought with me from Savannah was our Team-me t-shirt. Prior to becoming a head coach, I saw this shirt while attending a University of Georgia spring football coaches clinic. Their staff were wearing a t-shirt with the word TEAM written on the front. I brought that idea back with me but added a small "me" under the word TEAM. The t-shirt design had a side view of our helmet on the front. Above the helmet was TEAM written in big letters. Below the helmet was the word "me" written in small letters. The idea behind this shirt was to have our players realize that the team was bigger and more important than the individual.

All team personnel received their TEAM-me shirt prior to our first game. Everyone was expected to wear this t-shirt during our practice the day before all games. I always purchased extra TEAM-me shirts and handed them out to various school personnel and other people that contributed to the program. These extra shirts were usually given to administrators, secretaries, custodians, and TD Club officers.

I mentioned earlier that we had other ways of recognizing academic excellence. Being an educator, I stressed academics with my players. We started rewarding players for making the honor roll. We started recognizing players who made the honor roll after the fourth academic quarter. The fourth quarter grades were used to determine eligibility for the start of the season. Players making the fourth quarter honor roll received a t-shirt and a pair of shorts paid for by the TD Club.

Most seasons the first quarter ended before our season did. Another way of motivating players academically, was to recognize those making honor roll from the first quarter. The TD Club bought various articles of Vineyard clothing for those athletes.

One point I always made to parents of prospective players was that their son's grades would be higher during the football season than any other time of the school year. That was a fact, as we had more players making honor roll during the season than at any other time of the school year.

Without realizing it, the football program at Martha's Vineyard became well-respected, not only within our league but across the state. There isn't one particular area or event that I could place my finger on that earned us that distinction. Maybe it was our overall success. Perhaps it was how we treated our opponents. I think it was mostly the way our players competed and conducted themselves. The ultimate compliment I could ever receive from an opposing coach, win or lose, was that my team played hard.

Because of our success, the Vineyard was selected by the NFL to be one of eight high schools, nationwide, to appear in two halftime segments during Sunday Night Football in 2007.

The New England Patriots were enjoying an undefeated season that year. The two halftime shows where we appeared were during the Patriots back-to-back Sunday night games.

We played at Hull High School in Hull, Massachusetts. The crew from the NFL spent the entire week on the Vineyard interviewing and filming practices and local attractions. They traveled to the game on the boat and bus, filming as we went.

Coaches and players were mic'd up during the game, which we won.

Then, for the first and only time in my career, we received a police escort out of Hull.

The famous Lou Holtz, former college and NFL Head coach and former college announcer, once gave a great piece of advice. He recommended writing down your goals and when you obtain a goal, write down another one.

I took Lou Holtz's advice to heart. I retired knowing that I reached every goal I set. Those goals were both personal and team goals.

CHAPTER 31

"Perfection is not attainable. But if we chase perfection, we can catch excellence."
– Vince Lombardi

W hen I was in college and wanted to earn extra money, I joined the football officials association. I started attending meetings where we studied the rules, watched game videos, critiqued other officials, and discussed calls made during high school games.

Once the association felt I was ready, they gave me assignments to work games. I started off officiating youth football and was also assigned game clock duty at the high school level. It was during this time I gained an appreciation for the challenging work of the high school football official. Then again, if you asked any of my assistant coaches or former players, they might tell you an entirely different story.

Let's just say that during my tenure at Martha's Vineyard, I occasionally received extra privileges from several game officials. When most coaches were forced to stay close to their sidelines and off the field, I was often allowed to move about freely. There were times I would be seen standing on our near hash marks. I never interfered with a play or an official's ability to see, and if I had, I would have been rightfully penalized. Most officials allowed me to express my opinions more openly with them than other coaches.

There were, however, a few highly questionable calls that did not go our way. These calls did get reactions that some might say were somewhat out of character for me. One such call took place in my first year coaching on the Vineyard. We were playing our first home game of the season, the second game overall. The game was against an overmatched Cape Tech team from Harwich, Massachusetts. We were highly favored to win the game.

During the week of practice, we installed a trick play to use on our extra point. We already used a particular formation, the swinging gate. However, we prepared a play that would give us a chance for two points without actually lining up and showing our hand.

The holder for kicks that year was our junior QB/Safety, Todd Araujo. Todd was one of, if not, the most athletic players I coached. Our kicker was also a junior. Louis Paciello was our FB and played LB on defense. Louis was known more for his physical play than his kicking abilities.

In high school extra points and field goals are allowed to be kicked off a black tee. This is referred to as a kicking block. In order to kick off the block, it had to be brought or thrown onto the field before the snap of the ball. We used the tee as our deception.

After scoring a touchdown, the extra point team aligned in a regular formation, not our usual swinging gate. However, we did not bring the kicking tee onto the field. Once the head referee blew the ready for play whistle, my holder stood up, and started running towards our sideline yelling repeatedly, "Where's the tee? We need the tee!" In essence he was going in motion. I was on the sideline with both arms in the air. Once Todd had gone in motion far enough, I dropped one arm. That signaled Louis to have the center make a shotgun type snap to him. Once I saw the ball move, I dropped my other arm. The second arm drop signaled for Todd to stop and run down the sideline into the end zone.

Louis received the snap and threw a perfect pass to a wide open Todd Araujo in the end zone for two points. There were no defenders within ten yards of where Todd caught the ball. As we were celebrating this perfectly executed trick play, I looked over and saw a penalty flag on the ground. The head referee made some strange motion and called a penalty on us for deceiving the defense.

What?

I had never heard of such a penalty. I asked the official, "Are you kidding me? Isn't that what all offenses try to do on every play? Aren't all trick plays designed to deceive the defense?"

Nevertheless, the official walked off the fifteen yard penalty against us and we were forced to line up and go for two points. As I said, Louis was known as a physical player, not a kicker.

I don't recall if we made the two point conversion or not. We did, however, win the game comfortably. This game was my first win as the head coach on Martha's Vineyard. We never attempted the hidden tee play again.

Seasons came and seasons went. There were calls both good and bad. After cruising to an easy victory over Southeastern, we would play Weston in what would turn out to be our toughest challenge of the 1997 season. The coaches felt that by beating Weston, we could finish the season undefeated.

As it turned out, this game was everything we thought it would be and then some. The game was played on a windy, misty, Saturday afternoon. Weston's speed and athleticism matched ours. We were about as evenly matched as any two opposing teams could be.

The Vineyard took an early lead but had our extra point kick blocked. Weston responded and drove down the field and scored and made their extra point taking a 7-6 lead. On the ensuing kick-off, senior, Joel Graves, returned the kickoff for what was an apparent eighty yard touchdown return. During the return there were flags thrown behind the runner after Joel had crossed the goal line. We were called for an illegal block, even though there weren't any Vineyard players in the area of the flags. To make matters worse, Joel let his emotions get the best of him. Joel spiked the ball out of frustration over the bad call. The result was an additional fifteen yard penalty. We went into halftime down 7-6, the first time trailing that year. As the second half began, we marched down and got close enough to kick a field goal. Peter Lambos, our adept kicker, kicked a thirty yard field goal into the wind.

The game went back and forth with neither team able to mount an offensive drive. Then with about three minutes or less remaining in the game, Weston threw a pass toward our sideline. David Glassco, senior cornerback, intercepted the pass and was running down our sideline. Just as he got to where I was standing, he hurdled a Weston player that dove at his legs. At the same time, the chain gang threw their sticks onto the field into David's path. This action caused David to have to also hurdle the chains.

David never stepped out of bounds but the head linesman thought differently. Not only did he blow the call of David stepping out of bounds, neither he, nor any other official, threw an unsportsmanlike penalty on the chain gang. It took everything I had to keep my composure and not have a flag thrown against me. Realizing the importance of the situation played heavily into my deciding not to get a penalty against our team or me. We went on to win the game 9-7 and finished the season undefeated.

Football is a game that requires players and coaches to exhibit controlled emotion and intensity. The more competitive the game, the more control a player and coach must have. This philosophy was tested in our 2003 Super Bowl game against Manchester High School.

We entered this game with an 11-1 record. Our game with Manchester was a back and forth one. They took a seven point lead into halftime. We came out in the third quarter, and on our first possession drove the length of the field and tied the game at 14-14.

We held a 26-18 lead late in the fourth quarter and were one defensive stop away from securing the win. Manchester had some very talented, skilled players and an elusive QB who had been giving us fits all game.

There were two questionable calls that went against us on this last drive. On a critical third down play, their QB rolled out to his left after escaping two Vineyard pass rushers. He threw a pass toward his bench. John Valley, a senior linebacker, made a diving catch, keeping one foot in bounds, making what appeared to be a game clinching interception. The play caught the officials out of position and off guard. There were no referees near the spot of the catch to make the interception call. They ruled the play an incomplete pass.

We were now one play away from securing the victory. On the crucial fourth down play, the Manchester's QB, once again, scrambled away from our rushing defenders. He went to throw a pass but in mid-throw tried to stop his forward arm motion. The ball came out of his hand, hit the turf, and bounced right back to him. He gathered himself and threw a second forward pass into the corner of the end zone where one of his receivers made a great catch. The officials awarded them the touchdown.

These were two consecutive plays where, had any of the officials made the correct call, the game would have been over. We would have been able to simply take a knee and run out the clock.

As you may imagine, my players were dumbfounded and upset by the lack of professionalism shown by the officiating crew, as was my entire coaching staff. All of my attempts to get the official's explanations about both of Manchester's last two plays fell on deaf ears.

I was forced to take a time-out to let my players regain their composure before having to make a huge defensive play on Manchester's two-point conversion to tie the game. The score was 26-24, MV ahead, with about thirty seconds left in regulation. I guess what they say about karma being a bitch is true. We were in man to man coverage on the two-point play. One of their top receivers broke open on a pick route in the end zone. The QB threw a beautiful pass, hitting the receiver squarely in the hands. Fortunately for us, he dropped the ball.

Manchester attempted an onside kick, but we were able to make the recovery. We took our one knee and celebrated a hard-fought, Super Bowl victory over a well-coached and talented opponent.

This next situation occurred during one of our Island Cup rivalry games in 2011. We entered the last away game of our season as underdogs against a Nantucket team that was advancing to their postseason and would go on to win their Super Bowl a mere two weeks later.

Nantucket had a talented QB, senior, Taylor Hughes. This kid could do it all. In order for us to have a chance at winning, we would have to keep the ball out of Hughes' hands. The Vineyard had a good team this year, although our record of 4-6 at that point did not support that claim.

Before the Island Cup game, I installed a five play series out of the Double Wing offense, one that we called *tight*. We first ran this offense on the way to our Super Bowl win in 2003. If we could execute this scaled down version of the *tight* offense, it would help us sustain long drives, run the game clock, and keep Nantucket's high-powered offense off the field.

As luck would have it, Nantucket won the coin toss and received the kickoff. On their first play from scrimmage, Hughes reeled off a sixty yard gain, running the ball down to our six yard line. On their second play Hughes attempted a pass, but our inside linebacker, senior Michael Montanile, intercepted the ball inside our one yard line. Our first offensive possession would start from our half yard line.

We went on to a Vineyard history making, ninety-nine and a half yard drive. We had to convert a couple of fourth down plays in the process. This drive consumed thirteen and a half minutes of the game clock. With just under five minutes remaining in the first half, the Vineyard took an 8-0 lead. We held Nantucket to just five offensive plays in the first half. The Vineyard would get another two points as the result of a safety in the third quarter.

The questionable call took place late in the fourth quarter. MV had a 10-7 lead with about five minutes left. We needed to score a touchdown, because Nantucket had an outstanding field goal kicker. They also had the wind at their backs in this quarter.

Once again we were using our *tight* offense and driving. The Vineyard had a third down and one from the Nantucket one yard line. My QB that year was senior Delmont Araujo. Delmont was over 6 feet tall and weighed 210 pounds. I called for a QB sneak. To Nantucket's credit, they stopped Delmont short of the goal line. Now it was fourth down and under three minutes to play. I allowed the clock to run down and just before a delay of game penalty flag could be thrown, I called for a timeout.

We knew that if we punched the ball in for a score, the game was ours. Again, I called for a QB sneak. This time Delmont had half of his upper body across the goal line in the end zone. He held the ball up across the goal line for a touchdown. We all expected the officials to signal touchdown. To the surprise of everyone at the game, no signal was given. Even the chain gang of Nantucket backers, on our sideline, were shocked that we did not get credit for a touchdown.

Before Nantucket could snap the ball, I called another timeout. This time I wanted an explanation as to how my six foot tall QB could have half of his body in the end zone and no touchdown called. All the head referee, the late Bill Leanus, did was point to the side judges. Bill threw his crew under the bus by saying, "Donald, it's their call, not mine." Needless to say,

I was not happy with that explanation.

We went on to win the game 10-7. Senior CB Ryan Fisher intercepted a Taylor Hughes pass on our twenty-five yard line with under twenty seconds left to play. We took a knee and celebrated our ninth consecutive Island Cup victory.

Just when you think you've seen them all, there is one more surprise in store. One of the most bizarre, missed calls happened to us in 2013. We were playing at Fairhaven High School in Fairhaven, Massachusetts. This game was the first of three games the state assigned us due to the new playoff format. We did not qualify for the playoffs. The state selected three opponents for each team based on a power ranking system.

We took an early lead in the first half, going up 14-0. With just about one minute left in the second quarter, Fairhaven scored a touchdown, but we stopped their two point conversion attempt. We anticipated taking a 14-6 lead into halftime. Here is where it went terribly wrong.

After Fairhaven scored their touchdown, they kicked off to us. The kickoff went deep toward our best returner, senior DeShawn James. The ball was traveling fast and DeShawn was standing at the ten yard line. He allowed the ball to go past him stopping in the end zone. Nobody on our team touched the ball as it came to a stop in our end zone.

All of our players were coming off of the field, as the offense was starting to go onto the field. However, a Fairhaven player fell on the football. Instead of the official signaling touchback and giving us the ball at the twenty yard line, the head referee signaled touchdown.

Our entire sideline starting yelling, "It's a touchback, not a touchdown." As you may imagine I was very animated and insisted that the head referee come to me and explain his mistake. I expected that the referee was going to change the call to a touchback, which is the rule in this case for high school. The head referee called a huddle of his officials for a discussion. After fifteen to twenty seconds, the head referee came from his huddle and signaled, once again, touchdown.

I became animated all over again. This time, however, we had to regroup and put our defense on the field to stop their two point conversion attempt. We failed and Fairhaven tied the game 14-14 heading into halftime.

I was close to losing my mind yelling at the referees as we headed into our locker room. Fortunately we did go on to win the game by more than seven points, but that call has stayed with me all these years.

The Sunday night after our game with Fairhaven, we were at the house of Tom Keller, an assistant coach. We met at Tom's as a staff to review the previous game's film and game plan for the next opponent. Naturally, that ridiculous call was still on all of our minds.

At some point during that meeting, my cell phone rang and showed an unknown number. I answered the call to find out it was the head referee from the Fairhaven game. He called to apologize and finally admit that he blew the touchback call.

I accepted his apology but told him, "It's a damn good thing we didn't lose that game, or this conversation would have a completely different tone. But the thing that bothered me the most was the fact that all five officials missed that call. Why was it that when all of the officials got together to discuss the play and ruling, not one of you stepped up and said that the correct call was a touchback?" Unable to defend their position the referee apologized. I thanked him for the phone call.

Obviously many more controversial calls went against and in our favor while coaching at Martha's Vineyard. Most people, when they see me, don't think of me as a football coach. I am not your stereotypical looking football coach, for I am only 5'4" and weigh 150 pounds. I jokingly tell people that I used to be 6 feet tall, but the stress and pressure over the years caused me to shrink and turn my black hair a premature gray.

I always respected the tough job of high school football officials and appreciated their integrity and professionalism. Even though there were times I questioned their calls, I never felt as if my teams were being cheated. Part of my gamesmanship was to keep the referees on their toes.

I felt that I had a special relationship with most of the officials who worked our games. My teams were recipients of numerous Sportsmanship Awards from both the Mayflower League and the EAC, our two member leagues. As a result, when longtime, football official, Bill Leanus, passed away, I was the first recipient of the annual Bill Leanus Award for sportsmanship and mentoring young men in the game of football. This award was presented to me on behalf of the Eastern Massachusetts

Association of Interscholastic Football Officials.

I appreciated and respected the job Bill did as an official and considered him a friend. I have his plaque mounted on a wall in my house.

CHAPTER 32

"A trophy carries dust. Memories last forever." – Mary Lou Retton

At the beginning of the 2001 football season, my team moved from our practice field, located behind the game field, over to the track area behind the school. We made that decision because we could line off a regulation size football field inside the track. Before moving, the practice space we used was much shorter and narrower.

The only problem with this move was that there was a neighborhood close to the track. That would not impact us until after we started practice.

We were in the middle of one of our double session practices, one that started at 6:30 a.m. Halfway through that practice we were having a ten minute water break. As the players and I were enjoying the break, I looked up and saw a woman walking through the woods near the track. She was dressed in her pink bathrobe and slippers and was walking with a purpose in our direction.

I saw her approach one of my assistant coaches, Dan Rossi, who was a police officer for the town of West Tisbury. He pointed in my direction and the woman began walking my way. Not knowing what was going on, I started walking toward her.

As soon as I got close, the woman began yelling at me, "Excuse me, excuse me. Is there any reason your team has to be making this much noise this early in the morning? We love football but I have a two year old that is standing in his crib saying, hut, hut, hut. He's supposed to be sleeping right now."

After looking over at Dan Rossi and secretly thanking him for throwing me under the bus, I told her, "Yes, we need to be making this much noise." I did apologize for waking her son. Later that morning I received a call from my athletic director requesting that we start practice at 7:00 instead of the usual 6:30. Apparently we were in violation of the noise ordinance for the town of Oak Bluffs. The family even went so far as to contact the Superintendent of Schools about this issue.

Instead of moving the practice start time, we moved away from the neighborhood for the first thirty minutes of practice. At 7:00 we went back over to the practice field. We continued this routine for the remainder of that season.

For the next fourteen seasons we practiced at the track field. Eventually we would start our early morning practices by being as quiet as we could until 7:00 a.m. At the strike of 7:00, I would blow my whistle and the noise level increased.

In the 2015 season a young man by the name of Tucker McNeely was our starting quarterback. Tucker was a senior and in his third year of being involved in the football program. He did not play football as a sophomore. Tucker helped guide our team to a 7-4 record his senior year.

At our end of the year banquet I retold this story. When I recognized Tucker, I informed everyone at the banquet that it was Tuckers' mom, Jennifer Estabrook, who walked through the woods in her robe that morning. Tucker was the two-year old who had been yelling, "Hut, hut, hut." I had been waiting four years to tell this story and everyone in attendance had a good laugh, including Tucker.

CHAPTER 33

"Treat a person as he is, and he will remain as he is. Treat him as he could be, and he will become what he should be." - Jimmy Johnson

During my career I received numerous individual awards, won several championships, and have been the recipient of personal and team accolades. What I treasure the most are the letters and thank you notes from former players and parents, as well as the making of lifelong friendships. My former players, coaches, and I forged bonds that cannot be broken.

Jennifer Estabrook, mother of a former player, sent me the following:

"Donald Herman is an example of the kind of coach parents hope for and I'd like to use him to illustrate my points. Donald had a natural rapport with his players. He engendered respect out of desire and camaraderie, not out of fear or intimidation. While the ultimate goal was always winning the game, he understood the value of teamwork and good old fashioned fun. His approach to discipline was fair minded and consistent, never arbitrary, and there was never a fear of retribution. He managed to create a culture that we will forever be grateful for because Tucker built such strong relationships through that program and learned so many important lessons about life and about himself. Donald built a culture that nurtured the growth and development of the boys as football players but also as human beings."

For thirty-five years I taught and coached at the high school level with twenty-eight of those fulfilling years spent at the Martha's Vineyard Regional High School. I surrounded myself with outstanding people who were my assistant coaches. It was also my good fortune to have excellent young men play for me. They worked hard, were committed to my teaching, to each other, and to the football program. I enjoyed working in a wonderful community, one that accepted a born and bred southerner whom, for several years, people had a hard time understanding.

What I desired for my players was that they would learn the value of team sports and I tried to help mold young boys into caring men. I hoped my players would go on to become solid citizens who were role models, involved partners, husbands, fathers, and men who would make positive contributions to their communities and society.

I wanted my players to learn what sacrifice meant, what it was to have integrity, to be of solid character, and be able to face and overcome adversity. I wanted to make as big a difference in their lives as they made in mine.

Several of my athletes came from broken or splintered homes. The yearning the coaching staff and I felt for the players to feel a part of something important, led us to provide an environment where they felt safe, essential, and loved. Hopefully our team served as an oasis for such troubled young men.

Players often asked me to write them a college recommendation. I usually ended the recommendation with the following sentence, "(students name) always represented himself, his family, his school, and community in a first class way."

Retirement for me came in June of 2016 knowing that I did the best job possible for my team members, high school, and community on Martha's Vineyard. I retired with no regrets.

I'm also happy to say that I never woke up to a mysteriously placed "For Sale" sign in my yard.

ACKNOWLEDGEMENTS

If not for the encouragement from Jay Schofield, author of basketball and family history books, I don't believe I would have had the motivation to write this book. Jay also provided helpful suggestions along with Dan Sharkovitz, Kate Hennigan, Keith Dodge, Barbara Ardito, and Gail Herman. Without their input this book would have not been fit for publishing.

Thanks to Daniel J. Adams for the book cover layout and design and to the good folks at Kindle Direct Publishing for helping guide me through this self-publishing process.

Most of the photos were provided by Ralph Stewart, Michael Cummo, Sam Moore, David Welch, and assistance from Gabrielle Mannino at the MV Times. Also providing photos were Mark Alan Lovewell, Gus D'Angelo, Randi Baird and assistance from Hilary Wall at the Vineyard Gazette. Additional photos by Nicole Harnishfeger at the Nantucket Inquirer and Mirror, as well as the Cape Cod Times, Paul Cardoza, and David Araujo at DJR Photos were used.

Eric Herman, who tried teaching this old dog new tricks, helped with formatting, as did Louis Hall.

And last but not least, a heartfelt thank you to all the outstanding young men I coached over the years and to the many dedicated assistant coaches that sacrificed so much for Vineyard Football.

Made in the
USA
Middletown, DE